The Japan Sales Series

Japan Sales Mastery
Lessons from thirty years in Japan

Dr Greg Story
President, Dale Carnegie Japan

With a foreword by Dale Carnegie & Associates CEO Joe Hart

Dale Carnegie Training Japan
Tokyo
japan.dalecarnegie.com

FIRST EDITION

Foreword

Dale Carnegie is a global icon and a founder of the self-help world. Since the launch of his company in New York in 1912, his ideas and teachings have spread around the world. Dr Greg Story continues this by bringing the training to Japan, where Dale Carnegie Training commenced serving clients in Tokyo in 1963.

Dale Carnegie developed a sales course in 1939 with Percy Whiting, one of America's top salespeople. It was a revolutionary idea at the time. Until then, the only place you could get sales training was from your own company—if they had any to offer.

The textbook for the Dale Carnegie sales training course was updated in 1947 and titled *The Five Great Rules of Selling*. That course has been continually revised and refined over many decades, as it has been taught to salespeople around the world.

The Dale Carnegie sales methodologies have been adapted for the Japan market over the course of the past 50 years. Dr Story builds on that foundation, and this book is aimed at the non-Japanese salesperson, selling to Japanese buyers.

Dr Story has a unique background of having been selling into Japan since the 1980s, and in Japan since the early 1990s. He has a strong academic and language background, culminating in a PhD in Japanese studies. He has been a senior diplomat in Japan—having met Emperor Akihito three times—the country head of three large multinational organisations, the President of the Australian and New Zealand Chamber of Commerce in Japan, and is a sixth-degree black belt in traditional Japanese karate.

This book is the product of 25 years of insights and experience selling and leading sales teams in Japan. Dr Story is an acknowledged business thought leader in Japan, and I heartily recommend this book to all those who sell to Japanese buyers.

Joe Hart
President/CEO
Dale Carnegie & Associates

Preface

The great global fraternity of salespeople who sell face-to-face needs help, especially in Japan. If you work for a large Western company, you might get proper sales training. At a large Japanese company, the training is usually restricted to the infamous—and pretty much useless—OJT (On-the-Job Training). If you work for a small or medium-sized company, the likelihood of an internal training programme or investment in developing your sales abilities fades rapidly. You are expected to produce the goods and work it out by yourself. These companies use the rapid rotation method of bringing people in, scrutinising whether they can sell, then shipping them out if they can't.

There are plenty of excellent books on sales, but almost none on selling in Japan—certainly none that are current. This book is for my compatriots in the noble art and science of selling, particularly those hardy types selling in—or to—Japan. That said, the fundamental ideas, principles, frameworks, methodologies, and approaches work everywhere, because these are timeless and universal concepts. Also, in my experience, "if you can make it in sales in Japan, you can make it anywhere."

Japanese nationals have tremendous language and cultural advantages, but these alone are no guarantee for success. Being useless is no help, regardless of linguistic perfection. Dale Carnegie Training, founded in 1912 in New York, has been providing sales training in Japan for more than 50 years. We see plenty of salespeople in our classes—Japanese or otherwise—who have it unnecessarily tough. This is simply because they have no clue as to what they should be doing. They need help, guidance, and training. That is why I have written this book.

For foreigners working with Japanese buyers, language may or may not be an issue. Again, it doesn't help to speak Japanese well if you don't know how to sell. If you don't speak business-level Japanese, and so are restricted to selling only to English speakers, then you are excused on one level. You are still bound, however, by the cultural preferences of the Japanese buyer. This is a huge subject, and the focus of this book is not to provide a broad understanding of Japanese culture. There are many good books on this topic, so if you need insight into this area please get those as well.

This book focuses on how to sell to buyers, especially those who are Japanese or run businesses in Japan. It is aimed at you, the salesperson fighting it out every day on the front lines, but will also be useful to your Sales Leader boss in helping the sales team succeed. Often these bosses are untrained sales survivors, bridging economic downturns. They have managed to cling on, while others departed. It is never too late to learn and to gain useful ideas that can be passed on to those now on the front line of sales.

I have been selling to Japan since 1988, and have spent more than 30 years here altogether over three sojourns. I have been running Japanese sales teams and doing sales here myself, in the player/manager role, for the past 25 years.

I have always made it my practice, as a Sales Leader, to personally teach my sales teams. I wish I had discovered the Dale Carnegie method much earlier; we would have sold a lot, lot more!

Read this book, apply the Dale Carnegie method here in Japan, and brace yourself for much greater and faster success in sales.

Dr Greg Story
President
Dale Carnegie Japan

Greg.Story@dalecarnegie.com
www.dale-carnegie.co.jp

Acknowledgements

Writing this book about selling in Japan has been a labour of love. I am passionate about the subject of professionalism in sales, and want to help as many salespeople as I can make their sales life easier and more rewarding. I haven't done this on my own, because I have been helped by so many people. Let me list a few of the many for special thanks.

Joe Hart, CEO of Dale Carnegie & Associates, has been an inspiration for me. The way he leads our organisation is totally congruent with the Dale Carnegie human relations principles. Not many leaders actually walk the talk, but he certainly does.

We are all charged with carrying on the work that Dale Carnegie started. In 1939, Dale Carnegie worked with Percy Whiting, one of the most successful salespeople of his day, to create a sales training system to help salespeople. I have taken that system, which has been polished and refined over the many decades since, and highlighted its application for selling in Japan today.

The base of this book is drawn from the Dale Carnegie sales system, and we were extremely blessed in Japan to learn this system from a true master. Dave Stearns came to Japan to certify us as trainers in the sales training system, and his knowledge of sales—and his skill as a trainer—were both exceptional.

Clark Merrill and Ercel Charles are powerful thought leaders inside Dale Carnegie Training, and are both outstanding examples of the necessity to continuously strive for innovation in training.

There have been a number of sales leaders in Dale Carnegie Training around the world who I would like to recognise as inspirational role models of excellence. John Hei and Gerard Hei, in Taiwan, have shown all of us what is possible. Uwe Goethert, in Germany, has been a leader in very large account sales. Pallavi Jha, in India, has been an innovator who has grown that business enormously. And, in Minneapolis, Matt Norman and Mike Scott have pioneered new thinking about how to rapidly grow a training business, and have been very generous in sharing their knowledge.

I have also benefited from the wisdom of the greats of sales training: Charlie Cullen, J. Douglas Edwards, Frank Bettger, Joe Girard, Zig Ziglar, Brian Tracy, Tom Hopkins, Neil Rackham, Jeffrey Gitomer, and Grant Cardone. If you don't know these names, search them out. You will see that their knowledge has stood the test of time.

The students who have taken our sales course have been a tremendous source of inspiration, through the rapid progress they have made. They have contributed much to this book, through the issues they have flagged in the training and the areas of difficulty facing them in the real world of sales in Japan. In fact, it was their request for a book in English on selling in Japan that was the catalyst for this project.

Our Dale Carnegie trainers and staff in Japan have been fantastic in their dedication to an ideal started by Dale Carnegie. He was a man on a special mission, when it came to the quality of training delivery. We have made that mission our own true north to guide us here in Japan. The way everyone in our organisation here in Japan has embraced that idea is a credit to their professionalism and devotion to the cause Dale Carnegie started.

This book on selling in Japan languished for some time. I started, got about halfway through and then was distracted by other pressing demands on my time. Gary Vaynerchuk and his hustle philosophy got me off my backside and committed to finishing it.

My family has been a strong pillar of support. I have spent many hours at home writing and editing this book. I record my three weekly podcasts, work on our videos, and create the text content for daily posts in English and Japanese on LinkedIn, Facebook, and Twitter. This takes up a lot of time during evenings and on weekends. Without their understanding and support, I could never manage it all in addition to my full-time job running Dale Carnegie Training in Japan.

I would also like to thank the reader for taking the time to better understand the market in Japan and the intricacies of selling here. The basics of sales remains constant, but business itself is always evolving. I am sure there are other salespeople out there—selling to Japanese buyers—who will also have rich experiences and fresh insights about doing sales here. I look forward to hearing from you and sharing your Japan sales stories.

Thank you one and all.

Dr Greg Story
President
Dale Carnegie Japan

Table of Contents

Introduction

Selling in Japan has its own special flavour. There are differences compared with other countries, but they are not as great as you might imagine. Speaking Japanese obviously opens the door to a much bigger audience, but there are plenty of buyers who speak English. As pointed out earlier, language ability alone will not be the determinant of sales prowess. If it helps, most salespeople in Japan, be they foreign or local, are totally undertrained—or even untrained—and struggle every day as a result. So, you see, it is not just you!

My sales career started straight out of high school, with door-to-door encyclopaedia sales for Britannica in Brisbane in 1970. I was hopeless, by the way, and thought that I would never be any good at selling. After two stints in Japan as a postgraduate in the late 1970s and early 1980s, I returned to Australia in 1988 and started selling services, and later physical products, to Japanese corporations. Ironically, I ultimately joined a very large multinational company. What was their sales training methodology? OJT!

The stakes were very high, because these were big-ticket, multimillion-dollar items. It was at this point that I decided to take responsibility for my results and became a student of sales. I read widely on the subject, and began listening to cassette tapes (remember those?!) by the masters of selling. I was also able to attend a Tom Hopkins sales training rally in Brisbane. Importantly, I started to apply what I had read and heard. I changed careers, and moved back to Japan in 1992. I've been here ever since.

Japan is a big place. I have sold in Fukuoka, Kita-Kyushu, Hiroshima, Takamatsu, Koichi, Matsuyama, Fukui, Toyama, Kobe, Wakayama, Kyoto, Osaka, Nagoya, Gifu, Yokkaichi, Shizuoka, Tokyo, Sendai, Niseko, and Sapporo. Why do I take you on Greg's tour of Japan's provinces? Regional Japan is different from the capital, and I only fully appreciated how different after living outside of Tokyo for nine years. The ideas I present are based on my own experience on the front line of selling in Japan, on voracious study of the masters of selling, and on the 100-plus years of Dale Carnegie Training's insights into sales best practices.

The sales structure, the selling subtlety, the sales smarts, the nuances come from Dale Carnegie Training. Any system so continuously polished and improved over 100 years is certain to be deep, rich, and resilient. Dale Carnegie has been in Japan since 1963, so this is sales training *kaizen* on steroids!

Sales can be mechanical—if you see more people, you will make more sales. Know your ratios so that you know how many people you need to contact to know how much you will sell. All good stuff, but there is more to it than that. Having a sound sales philosophy helps provide a holistic approach that builds a sustainable professional career. Yes, a career!

Sales gets smeared with negative images of dodgy con artists and hucksters fleecing rubes. There are criminals in all professions, but sales in particular has an air about it. This is bizarre, really, because as the old business wisdom teaches, "nothing happens until a sale is made."

Sales is the driving force of commerce and society. Sales of ideas, concepts, initiatives, services, and physical products are the lifeblood of human progress. We are all in sales—to some degree—although most people don't think of themselves that way.

"What do you think of this approach?" "I recommend we do this project." "I have an idea for this year's budget." "Shall we have lunch?" These are all statements with which we are trying to sell something to someone. Whether we realise it or not, we are all selling something to someone else every day.

We can't take personal responsibility for idiots, shysters, criminals, lowlifes, boiler room riffraff, pond scum, or other unscrupulous types lurking in sales, but we can take full responsibility for our professional selves. We don't want to be "good at sales." We want to be "good people who sell." This starting point is so important and so different. If we choose the latter, we can each hold our head up high, and build a long and successful professional career in sales.

First, take a moment and determine just WHY you are in sales? This is the most fundamental, yet critical, question we need to address. Often, we just get into sales without really thinking about our WHY. Are you here primarily to serve your own interests or to serve the client's interests? The answer to that question makes all the difference.

To build a professional career in sales, we need to understand that our success is a direct consequence of our client's success. My firm advice is to completely believe that what you are selling is good for the client. If not, then stop what you are doing and go find something you can believe in. Your WHY—and how much you believe in what you are doing—defines you.

Become a professional, make sure you have a clearly mapped-out sales process, arranged in distinct phases. This will ultimately lead to the destination: the first of many sales. We are not in sales to achieve just a single sale. We are here to totally satisfy our buyer, to the extent that they continue to buy from us forever. Keep this in mind. We are not after a sale, but after reorders.

If you don't know how to ask clients truly brilliant questions, then learn or leave sales. Telling isn't selling, and BS no longer baffles brains. Understand the question build process and the different communication patterns needed to be successful.

Presenting the solution is a sophisticated procedure, and disciplined clarity is required.

If, for whatever reason, the questioning component of the sales process wasn't complete enough, we need to get off the back foot, dig deep to recover, and deal with the issues raised by the client. Not everything goes in a straight line, so knowing how to do that properly is essential.

Finally, ask for the order! If you follow the advice in this book, you will have earned the right and will be fully confident to do so.

In these pages, I cover the face-to-face sales process from beginning to end. I am going to include some simple ideas on the pre-sales preparation. In this era, we have so much information available to us about companies and the individuals we are going to meet. It is incredible. Through online annual reports, Google, Yahoo, Facebook, Twitter, LinkedIn, Wikipedia, etc., the internet has opened the floodgates of information—all you have to do is look for it.

I am going to cover the after-sales process, although this will vary so much depending on what you sell. Follow through must be done well. To understand the importance of this point, fully consider the lifetime value of the customer.

What does this mean?

If your client's first purchase was only $50,000 this year, you may not consider them a high-profile client. However, if they keep buying from you for ten years, this client is actually worth $500,000 not $50,000. That is their real lifetime value as a buyer.

If we deal with our clients from the point of view of making them successful, and have in mind that "wrapped in their success is our success," then we will naturally want to build a lifetime relationship. I try to make my clients my friends, because I want my world to be made up of people I like and who like me.

This is how Japanese buyers approach the relationship. They prefer the devil they know to the angel they don't. They won't easily switch suppliers for a few pennies. This is not ironclad but, generally speaking, once you are in and you look after the buyer, you tend to stay in.

After establishing your clear WHY, make this concept of the lifetime value of the customer the starting point for how you think about building the client relationship over time. Consider how you can go the extra mile before being asked. This will have positive ramifications for creating both your personal brand as a sales professional and your business success.

1—Keep Your Shtick to Yourself Buddy

Smoothly memorised shtick, elaborate glossy materials, sharp suits, large expensive watches, bleached teeth, and the perfect coiffure are not important in sales. Yet, this is the image of the pro-salesperson. Most of us never meet many of these "pro-sales-people," because the vast majority of the salespeople we run into are hopeless. We meet the great unwashed and untrained, the part-time and partially interested, usually in a local retail format.

The slick sales dude is what we see in movies, or is an image from urban myths. Hollywood pumps out films such as *Wall Street*, *Glengarry Glen Ross*, *Boiler Room*, and *The Wolf of Wall Street*, in which we are sold an image of what high-pressure salespeople look like.

Japan is fascinating, in that it throws up some doozies. Rotting blackened stumps for teeth, dishevelled clothing, scuffed worn shoes, ancient food stains on ties—you encounter this low level of personal presentation here with salespeople. It is almost the opposite extreme of the urbane, polished American Hollywood movie image.

Rat with a gold tooth or rat with a rotting tooth—neither appeal very much. What buyers really want is someone who is on their side. They want help solving issues that are slowing them down, holding them back, or preventing them from growing as they wish. There are six steps on the client journey with salespeople:

1. Know you
2. Like you
3. Trust you
4. Buy from you
5. Repeat buy from you
6. Refer you, because they are a fan and a believer

This sounds simple, but some salespeople get confused about who they are working for. They think they are there to work for

themselves and get their commission, bonus, or promotion. The
client is just a tool in that process. This is stupid.

DUMB THINGS SAID

I coach salespeople, but am amazed at the dumb things they say
and do. Some want to jam the square peg in the round hole and
then argue with the client about why it will fit when it clearly
doesn't. When they get pushback from the client, they try to
overwhelm the objection by will or force of personality. This is
stupid, too.

The salesperson grabs their laptop and jumps into the slide
presentation from the get-go, without asking a single question
of the buyer. Or they are pulling out their shiny flyers or
expensive brochures—or whatever—and launch forth with their
memorised shtick.

As I mentioned in the introduction, my first sales job was
early-evening, door-to-door Britannica encyclopaedia sales in a
poor, working-class suburb in Brisbane. Before we were unleashed
on an unsuspecting semi-literate public, we had to memorise word
for word the entire twenty-five-minute presentation. Even then, as
a sales methodology, it wasn't great; but in this modern era it is
unacceptable. Some people are still stuck back in the 1970s with
their sales efforts. I still get calls today from overseas call centres
telling me "so and so" is in my area, etc. I can hear the cadence of
them reading it off a script! We have some way to go to see everyone as a sales professional.

NO MORE SHOW AND TELL

When I am coaching aspirant professional salespeople, I ask them
what they do now. Invariably, they whip out their materials and
plough right in with their canned speech. I ask them how they
know which slides to show or which flyer they should offer to the
client. This is usually greeted with, "Huh, what do you mean?"

We all did "show and tell" in elementary school, but some
have not travelled very far since and think this is how you do

sales. This is the fault of organisations that don't properly train their sales teams. When I began working at Shinsei Retail Bank in Tokyo, the financial product sales team would whip out a flyer of one product. If the wealthy individual client didn't go for it, then they would just whip out the next one. This went on until the client either got tired or bought something. It was completely crazy, and I spent four years there fixing it.

Here is a golden rule to abide by: As salespeople, we don't know what to show the client; and we shouldn't show the client anything until we know what they want. So, keep the laptop closed, the flyers in the briefcase, the widget under the table, and ask well-designed questions instead. By the way, get permission to ask questions first—especially in Japan. Here, the status of the buyer is sky-high, and it is a total impertinence for lowly sales pond scum to be asking the Buyer God questions about anything.

GET PERMISSION
Nevertheless, get permission and ask. Find out if there is a match. Mentally scour the walls of your gigantic solutions library, packed floor to ceiling with possible antidotes to their business ailments, and select the best one for the client. If there is no solution in your library, don't try and force the square peg into the round hole. Just thank them for their time and go find someone you can help.

If your solution doesn't fit, don't waste the client's time. Keep your shtick to yourself. Better still, ditch the shtick entirely. Study the twin arts of designing great questions and listening. I mean really listening, not just fake listening.

ACTION STEPS

1. Realise you work for the client's interests, not your own.
2. Don't get into an argument with the client; you will never win.
3. We will investigate your sales philosophy in the next chapter, so start thinking about what that might be.
4. Don't memorise your presentation and just deliver that content regardless of what the client may need.
5. Don't show the client anything until you know what they want.
6. Don't think that telling has anything to do with selling.
7. If your solution is not a fit, get out of there quickly and find another buyer for whom it is.

In the next chapter, we will look at developing your Sales Philosophy.

2—What Is Your Sales Philosophy?

D o we need a sales philosophy to be successful in this profession? I think we do. Like a lot of people, I subscribe to various sites that send you useful information, uplifting quotes, etc. The following morsel popped into my inbox one morning:

> *People don't care how much you know,*
> *until they know how much you care.*
> *—Anonymous*

Wow! What a powerful reminder of the things that really matter in our interactions with others. This piece of sage advice should be metaphorically tattooed on the brain of every single person involved in sales.

Don't miss it—we all know selling stuff is a tough gig. Rejection is the normal response to our spiffy sales presentation and follow-up offer. They choose your competitor over you, for all or a part of the project. Ouch! You have to be mentally tough to survive in a sales job. You need other things, too. Product and technical knowledge is important. This is a given. Your total command of the micro details is expected by clients, especially in data-hungry Japan. Fine. However, we need to be careful about what we focus on. Are we letting perfect knowledge of the product details and features confuse us about what selling is really all about? What is the main game? What is our philosophy toward this sales life?

Reading the previous paragraph may sound a bit ephemeral, rather fluffy to some. Fair enough, but let me ask: If you don't have your own philosophy towards sales, then just what do you have? Just what are you using as the "light on the hill," guiding the path forward? As a sales professional, how do you hold all the internal and external contradictions and inconsistencies together? What is your level of self-awareness? What are you really on about, with this sales lark of yours?

As a buyer, many salespeople I have encountered remind me of an icy mammoth trapped in a time warp from the past, still trotting out the product brochure and seeing if I will go for one of their goodies. You don't like that one? Well, then, how about this one? Or this one? Or this one? *Ad nauseam.* I want blue, but they keep showing me 50 shades of pink. They are playing that untrained, pathetic, failed salesperson game called Russian Roulette Process of Elimination.

When I joined Shinsei Retail Bank in 2003, this is what I discovered our hardy salespeople were doing. The wealthy client would sit down and then be treated to a firestorm of flyers promoting one financial product after another. Sadly, no questions were being asked to understand their concerns, aspirations, time frames, values, or goals. It was hopeless and ultimately unsuccessful. We soon turned that situation around and sales really took off.

As the client, I want to buy; but I don't want to be sold to. These types of "product push" salespeople prove to the buyer that they are not focused on understanding what is needed. Are they joining in the conversation going on in my buyer head? Are they demonstrating that their foremost concern is my benefit? Are they communicating to me that, "In your success, Greg, is my success"? Nope. Instead, they come across not with stars in their eyes, but with ¥¥¥ signs.

At different times over the past 25 years in Japan, I can recall seeing these people sitting across the table from me, mentally salivating at the thought of the big fat commission this sales conversation is worth. I can sense they have already mentally bought a BMW 3 Series before the ink is dry on our agreement. This will not end well and is a formula for tears before bedtime for salespeople.

The quote at the beginning, "People don't care how much you know, until they know how much you care," reminds me of the great Japanese expression *kokorogamae* (心構え), which is made up of two words: *kokoro* (heart) and *kamae* (stance). This should be embraced by everyone as a solid philosophical approach to this business of sales.

It can be simply translated as "spiritual preparedness," but the Japanese nuance goes much deeper. Anyone studying a martial art or a traditional Japanese art (道, *michi*) will immediately be on my wavelength when they hear the term *kokorogamae*.

You will see it in the master's seated meditation in the dojo before the start of martial arts training, the *ikebana* master stripping the stems and leaves by hand before making the flower arrangement, the *shodo* (calligraphy) master laboriously rubbing the ink stone themselves before taking up the brush and writing a beautiful character. These masters all do this to get their mind prepared for what they are about to create.

As a side note, here is a little Japanese language insight for you. *Kokoro* means your heart or spirit. *Kamae* means your ready position. In karate, for example, we take our *kamae*, or fighting position, when we do free sparring. The word *kamae* becomes gamae when *kokoro* and *kamae* are combined into a single compound word. We can translate *kokorogamae* as "getting your heart in order." This *kokorogamae* concept is one of the core foundations of my life philosophy.

For salespeople, rather than "spiritual preparedness" or "getting your heart in order," I would prefer to translate *kokorogamae* as "getting your intentions in order." If that sounds a bit too esoteric, let me explain where I am going with this idea.

Kokorogamae means to hark back to your most basic philosophical principles of WHY, of choosing a direction and taking action. That direction is what we can call True North—the purity of our intention that determines our subsequent actions. What is the initial spark in our heart that is driving our behaviour? What are our values, which in turn determine our behaviour? Is it the pursuit of money or the pursuit of serving? Is it what you want to harvest or is it building a profession by providing what the client wants? Is this going to be a long-term relationship or a fleeting, smash-and-grab transaction?

> *The choices we make impact the actions we take,*
> *which determine the harvest we reap.*
> *Salespeople need to start by searching*
> *their heart for their WHY, their true intentions.*

Whoa! Does this still sound a bit too "hug a tree" Californian style, overly emotional for you? Why do I recommend searching your heart? This isn't about becoming misty-eyed and emotional. This is pure pragmatism and logic. Clients are not stupid; they can sense when our motivation isn't centred on their best interests, and therefore they won't buy from us or—much more importantly—continue to buy from us. Let's be crystal clear: you are not after a sale, you are 100% committed to satisfying the client, so that there are reorders.

When we figure in the lifetime value of a customer, we can see the short-term gain of a single sale for what is: the most expensive sale we will ever make. I am not recommending Hollywood-style faking interest in the customer's benefit to hook a sale. I am talking about genuinely having the customer's gain at the forefront of all our decisions.

I said that the customer will not buy from us if our intention is miscued; but, of course, there are exceptions. The movie image of the smooth-talking salesperson who could sell you anything, and will certainly try to, is powerful. *Wall Street, Boiler Room, Glengarry Glen Ross,* and *The Wolf of Wall Street* all portray the buyer as the patsy, conned by Mr Smooth. These salespeople are like skyrockets that initially blaze through the night and then explode! They are here for a good time, not a long time.

They may con us once, but we will eventually work them out. In this modern technological age of handheld devices and 24/7 global connectivity, social media can kill us very quickly. Our reputation in the market can be shredded and, before we know it, we are out of business. In the old days, you might tell five people about how you were duped by a salesperson. Today, with the press of a button, you can warn millions of people to be wary.

I saw this upfront and personal in a broad-spray LinkedIn post from Person A, whom I know here in Tokyo, raising a complaint about not getting paid by Person B, whom I also know. I was thinking, "Wow, Person B's reputation is being publicly trashed in the market in a very damaging way." What did I do next? I Googled Person B and found a lot of other very worrying stuff.

By the way, it happened that we were in talks with Person B about some collaboration. Guess what? We broke off the talks; and that is what will happen to all of us if we do the wrong thing. It will instantly get shared far and wide through social media land.

Bad people in sales give us and the profession a bad brand reputation. We must be squeaky clean to compensate for all the bad press the profession draws. Remember, I said we have to be good people in sales, not good salespeople!

As a Sales Leader, the most highly skilled Japanese salesperson I ever interviewed for a sales job was a criminal. The criminal part didn't surface immediately, but came up later through background checks. (Note to Sales Managers: Do background checks!)

He was absolutely brilliant in the first two interviews—polished, genius personified in the role play, and WOW, what a closer!

I thought "Yes! At last, I have found my perfect Japanese salesperson." Actually, he was a polished liar, a thief, and a baddie. He had zero True North orientation and his *kokorogamae* was just plain wrong. What a wake-up-and-smell-the-coffee moment for me.

So, let's ignore the outliers, the riffraff and pond scum of sales, and come back to the vast majority of salespeople who are not evil, just struggling because they are untrained and have no central philosophy or WHY clarity about what they are doing in sales. They are underskilled because they have never received proper sales training. People often arrive in sales jobs through companies that are transactional in nature. It is the industrial model of sales.

Potential salespeople come in the front door and, if they don't magically hit their numbers, are shown the back door after a few weeks or months. Another sacrificial victim is then brought in through the front door and the process repeated forever.

No thought is given to investing in these new hires to properly develop their understanding and skills. It is just a throw of the dice every time, to see who stays and who goes.

This routine usually produces very unfortunate sales behaviour in the individuals involved, as they become more and more desperate to make a sale to keep their job. Desperation drives people to extremes, and the client's interests in all of this are thrown out the window. The ethos of the organisation is short-term gain, and their salespeople are a type of plug-and-play item to be switched out as soon as it fails.

Change your heart, focus on True North, purify your intentions, show that you genuinely care about the buyer's best interests before your own. If you do that every single time you meet a client, you will have great success in sales and build a powerful personal brand based on trust.

You want buyers to know, like, and trust you. Establishing our individual sales philosophy based on the *kokorogamae* true intention concept will deliver the like and trust components in spades. If your current sales life is a nightmare of transactional relationships, burning clients for short-term gain, unrelenting pressure on the numbers, and no training, then get out of there as soon as possible.

Well-trained, capable salespeople are always in demand. Stop wasting your time with a loser employer and get your career on the road to success.

Take responsibility for yourself, make *kokorogamae* your light on the hill, and move forward. Watch videos on YouTube, get the books on sales written by the famous masters, and study hard about what it takes to have a successful sales life. Apply what you learn and keep polishing.

If you want to stay in sales, then create your own philosophy of what that means to be the very best that you can be. Decide what your personal *kokorogamae* of sales will be. No more hesitation; let's commit and get on to it!

Trust is the magic ingredient in business, and the way to succeed in sales is to recreate that trust every time—in every interaction—with the client. This is particularly important with our best clients. We can easily become complacent, taking them for granted because the relationship is so strong. Don't do that. Make this your mantra instead:

> *I focus on my WHY I am in sales, my* kokorogamae.
> *I will not be complacent. I have to recreate the trust with each client in every interaction.*

ACTION STEPS
Start at the start …

1. Set your direction based on your philosophy of sales.
2. Determine your *kokorogamae* and never be tempted to stray from the true path you have set.
3. Seek to establish long-term relationships built on trust.
4. Genuinely care about your client.
5. Remember, in the client's success lies your own success.

In the next chapter, we will look at the importance of belief in what you are selling and its impact on your sales success.

3—Creating Sales Certainty

T he hardest sales job in the world is selling something you don't believe in. The acid test is: Would you sell this "whatever" to your grandmother? If the answer is no, then—as I said in the last chapter—get out of there right now! But it is rarely that clear-cut. The more important test is whether what you are selling solves the client's problem. Selling clients on things that are not in their best interest is a formula for long-term failure, as well as personal reputation and brand *seppuku* (suicide).

There are elements of the sales process that are so fundamental that you wonder why I even bring them up. For example, believing in what you sell. There are lots of salespeople, though, trapped in jobs where they don't believe, yet they must keep selling to pay the rent and put food on the table for their families. They may be working in an environment where "screw the client" is the dominant culture, where everything is purely transactional and based on a "one and done" approach to the relationship. Often, the official company rhetoric is all about the importance of the customer but, when the economy tanks, those high-blown sound bites sail out the window and it becomes company first, customer last.

You don't have to look far to find these "one and done" salespeople. They are going through the motions but, as the client, you never feel they have your best interests at heart. They usually don't have any other sales process than blarney and BS. They can be really good talkers, and we may buy from these people once; but we come to bitterly resent being conned and we don't forgive or forget. In Japan, companies are really excellent at record keeping across the generations of staff position rotations within the firm. They don't leave it to memory to keep track of the bad guys.

I used to get "sales" faxes from Nigeria promising me millions if I would just park a humungous amount of their money in my account for a while. Then the faxes changed to emails, and lately I am getting munificent offers through Facebook and LinkedIn.

In fact, Merv A King, supposed ex-Governor of the Bank of England, sent me a cheery note through LinkedIn about a small problem he has with £20,600,000 in his bank, and how I can get 40% if I help him out. It is a well-trodden scam, but these criminals operate on the basis that there is a proportion of greedy people out there who will fall for this and get conned. They know their "sales" ratios! These are extreme criminal con artist cases, and they are not going away anytime soon. Remember, everyone gets these, so there is always a question in the back of the buyer's mind: Can I really trust this salesperson?

The more common problem with salespeople is not that they are criminals or con artists. They actually do believe in what they sell, but they are not very good at selling that idea. Sadly, they are not professional enough to be convincing in the sales conversation.

They often have a "sales personality" deficiency, where they are not good with people or not good with different types of people. They get into sales by accident. In many cases, they should have been screened out at the selection stage; but sadly the world is just not that logical.

When I joined Shinsei Retail Bank, I recognised straight away that 70% of the salespeople should never have been given a sales role. They, through no fault of their own, were in the wrong job. My brief was "we have 300 salespeople and we are not getting any-where—come in and fix it." The vast majority of salespeople in the role of convincing wealthy Japanese customers to buy our Shinsei financial products were really suffering.

They lacked a sales philosophy, the communication skills, the people skills, the persuasion power, the warmth, the concern for the customer, etc., that they needed to be successful. Why on earth were they there then, you might ask?

Many of them had never been in a sales role. Many had been in backroom jobs, never facing customers. When Shinsei Retail moved all the operations components out of the branches, they gained tre-mendous efficiency and cost savings. The operations part became centralised in the IT headquarters in the Tokyo ward of Meguro, and it worked like a charm; but the operations staff were left there in the branches and given sales jobs. Disastrous for them! How about your own case right now? How is your current sales environment? Are your colleagues in the right role? Are you in the right role?

At Shinsei, we worked out who was best suited for a sales position—serving wealthy customers—and gave those people the proper training to equip them for success. The remainder of the staff were given roles more suited to their skills, elsewhere in the bank.

In many Western countries, they would probably have been fired. Although this can be crushing for the individuals involved, at some point trying to slam the square peg into the round hole has to stop. Einstein's definition of insanity was to keep doing the same thing but to expect a different result! If sales is not for you, then change careers or change yourself and develop the skills you need to be successful.

What training did we give them? Before I arrived, the Retail Bank HR team thought that mathematics ability was really important when recruiting and selecting bankers. It probably was for certain roles, but the ability to ask good questions, to fully understand wealthy customer's needs, fears, and long-term goals was much more important.

We were selling investment products: mutual funds, annuities, bonds, real estate investment trusts (REITs), and various other elaborate constructs. Conceptual products like this have no smell, can't be seen, can't be touched, make no sound, and have no taste. Faith in what you are being told is central to handing over your cash in exchange for one of these intangible investment ideas. Trust is paramount.

If I don't like you or trust you, why would I want to buy anything from you? So, first impressions should not be left to chance. They need to be crafted. Most salespeople never have a firm strategy for their first impressions. If you have a solid sales philosophy, based around your *kokorogamae* of serving the customer's best interests, then you will pass the first impression test, gain trust, and be successful in sales.

At Dale Carnegie Training, we do a lot of sales training for corporate clients, and we see the same issues with their salespeople coming up constantly. There are some fundamental errors being made. Fortunately, they are not hard to fix.

Certainty around the thing being sold must be in evidence. Here is another sales mantra for you:

> **Selling is the transfer of your enthusiasm for the product or service to the buyer.**

Your natural body language must exude belief. Your face needs to be friendly. Ancient Chinese wisdom observed that "a man who can't smile should not open a shop."

This may sound a bit ridiculous—what's the big deal about smiling? Well, many people in sales roles don't smile easily. They don't exude warmth, coming across as cold, hard, mercenary, and overly sharp and efficient (to aid themselves).

Here is a hint for leaders of sales teams: Japanese people can be very serious, earnest, and well intentioned. However, that serious face can sometimes look unfriendly. How about your own face when you are really concentrating? Does it look friendly to the viewer?

First impressions count. "How are you today?" is a pathetic sales call opener, made even more dismal when delivered in a flat, uninterested monotone voice. Whether face to face or on the phone, it is a dud. You would think no one in their right mind would try to start a sales conversation in that way, but sure enough they do.

Because we buy services and we speak English, I have suffered a series of these obnoxious openings. I wondered who on earth was tutoring them to begin with this flawed approach? "Fake" doesn't even begin to describe that vital first impression.

We all love to buy, but we hate being sold to; and at the other end of the scale, "really efficient" salespeople make us very nervous. They are too smooth. We worry we are being outfoxed, that we are now swimming with sharks. Anything that is not grey with lots of teeth is prey, and we realise that is us. Being "genuine" rather than "clever" or "cunning" is what we are looking for in successful salespeople.

Fluency in communication is also critical. Be it in Japanese or English, a lot of "filler words," such as *eeto, anou*, uhm, and ah, might help you think of what you want to say next, but in sales you come across as unsure or unconvinced about what you are saying or proposing. We, the prospect, definitely don't buy salesperson uncertainty. If you don't seem to believe what you are saying, why should we?

By the way, allow me a small digression, because here is a simple One-Point Lesson on how to kill the *eeto*s, *anou*s, uhms, and ahs forever. Practice this in normal conversation first, rather than practicing on the client!

1. Think of what you are going to say, hit the very first word hard and, when you get to the end of the sentence, purse your lips together.
2. Think of the next thing you are going to say, hit it hard and, at the end of the sentence, purse your lips together.
3. Repeat this every time you open your mouth to speak— and you will eliminate the filler words completely.

Hesitancy in speech is a killer of sales. At the other end of the spectrum, a totally canned sales speech is a disaster, too. I mentioned earlier that I was a failed encyclopaedia salesman for Britannica, as my first sales job in the early 1970s. You might recall that I noted how we aspirant salespeople had to pass a memory test in which we would recite the entire 25-minute presentation word for word. Each sales conversation stanza was linked to a specific page in the glossy sales presentation materials.

Having passed the recall test, we were dropped off in a forlorn, working-class outer suburb of Brisbane and turned loose on an unsuspecting public. There were few questions involved, but a tremendous lot of data-dumping going on in that canned speech.

I was hopeless. I thought I would never be any good in sales after that miserable experience. I was young and tender, failing to realise that the way we were doing it was hopeless.

Astonishingly, despite all we know 40-plus years later, there are still people trying to make a career in sales while wading through minute after minute of the data dump of the features.

Where are the questions for the client, the understanding of needs, the explanation of the benefits of the features, the application of the benefits, the evidence that this has worked for others? In other words, the proper sales basics. It is not complicated.

Success in sales is rooted in following a process based on three powerful foundations:

1. Your own belief in what you are selling is in the best interest of the client
2. Your ability to fluently articulate back to the buyer what you just heard that they need, and to check that you have properly understood them
3. Your ability to explain clearly how your solution is the best match to satisfy their need

We must sell ourselves first before we start bothering clients with the details. Take a mental audit of yourself right here and now. Are you a believer or a faker?

ACTION STEPS
If you want to be successful in sales, make sure you get …
1. a proper sales philosophy
2. a solid sales process
3. certainty
4. fluency
5. going!

In the next chapter, we will craft our credibility statement so that the client will know, like, and trust us.

4—Credibility Is King in Sales

Salespeople are carrying around a lot of baggage when they visit clients. As we have noted, the smooth-talking, dodgy salesperson who tries to con everyone is the folkloric villain of the piece. Reversing that doubt and hesitation is critical to gaining acceptance as a valuable business partner for the client. This entire trust problem is magnified when we meet the client for the first time.

Because the client doesn't know us, their default position is one of caution and doubt. We have all grown up being rewarded for being averse to risk, and that is why we are so resistant to change. The new salesperson represents change because they are asking the client to buy something new or to switch suppliers. There was a famous American television commercial in the 1980s in which the punch line was: "No one ever got fired for buying IBM." This is exactly the mentality of the risk-averse Japanese buyer: Go with the known and avoid any personal career risk.

A Japanese buyer is usually a so-called *salaryman* (long-term salaried employee), and has learnt firsthand that Corporate Japan does not place a premium on initiative over avoiding risk.

The Japanese love affair with risk aversion and the structure of internal career progression absolutely drives the *salaryman* to stay with the known over the untested and unproven.

If you are trying to sell into that company for the first time, you are unknown, untested, and unproven; therefore you are automatically in the high-risk category! "Guilty until proven innocent" is the flavour of your sales interview in Japan. To properly serve clients, we need to break through the mental protective wall that has been erected to keep us at bay and quickly establish trust and credibility.

Great! But how do we do that?

We need to craft a Credibility Statement. This is a succinct summary that will grab the attention of the client and help to reduce their resistance to what we are offering.

It unfolds in four stages:

1 We give an overview of the general benefits of what we do. For example:

"Dale Carnegie Training helps to deliver the mind-set and behaviour changes needed in the team to produce improved results."

2 We need to quote some specific results as evidence that we are a credible supplier of services. When we do this, we need to include a reference to the problem the client was having. In this way, we can provide context around the viability of the solution. So, we now might say something like this:

"An example of this was where we helped a very high-end retailer train their entire sales staff. They were getting nowhere, and now they are reporting to us that they are enjoying a 30% increase in sales."

This has to be a verifiable fact, by the way, not just hot air and bluster.

3 We now suggest that this benefit and result are relevant for the buyer.

"Maybe we could do the same for you."

This sounds like a very simplistic statement, but it is very subtle and very powerful. There is no hard sell going on here. In fact, it is best delivered with neutral body language and in a tone of voice that is rather matter-of-fact. We actually don't know if we can help them yet, but we sure want to find out.

4   We need to create a "verbal bridge," so that we can move on
to questioning the client about what they really need. We will
deal with this in a moment.

In Japan, a lot of buyers expect to control the proceedings.
When the seller turns up, they are there just to give their pitch.
Then the buyer mentally loads the double-barrel shotgun and pro-
ceeds to shoot the pitch full of holes.

What Japanese buyers are doing is trying to ascertain the risk
factor of what you are proposing by disparaging everything you
have just said. They now want you to provide solid answers that
eliminate their fears.

Believe me, this is bad.

You are now immediately shunted on to the back foot. You
are under attack, and incoming ordnance is raining down on your
head. The client, not you, is controlling the sales process. Sales
brothers and sisters, good luck with that approach!

Every single time I have been forced to just give my "pitch"—
because the buyer has denied me the opportunity to ask questions—there has been no sale achieved. You do your best and go
through the motions, but deep down you know this is a suicide
mission for which the only outcome is "result oblivion." By the way,
I hate that!

We need to get clients to allow us to better understand how
we can best serve them. That is why we must get permission to ask
questions and then listen very, very carefully to the answers.

To break this "pitch first" pattern—which has an abysmally
low success rate—we need to ask pertinent questions and find
out what the client really needs. In order to do that, we need their
permission to ask questions in the first place. This transition into
the questioning part of the sales process is absolutely critical.

In the Japanese hierarchy, the buyer is God and the salesperson is just pond scum. Japanese buyers, trained to massacre sales
pitches, feel our questions are impertinent, presumptive, rude, intrusive, and unnecessary; so we must gain their permission to proceed.

If we don't set up permission for the questioning component, we may find ourselves sitting there high and dry, facing stony silence as they ignore our questions or give unhelpful, perfunctory answers. In my experience, gained from doing it the wrong way, I have found Japanese buyers to be pretty good at playing the role of sceptic. A dark, scowling, impatient face normally accompanies all of this—and can certainly ruin your day.

If your buyer is not Japanese, it is still sound practice to seek permission to ask questions. Remember, we are just walking in off the street and wanting to ask them the most intimate details about all the pain points in their business. Not everyone wants to share that type of sensitive information with a total stranger whom they just met five minutes ago.

To get the sales process back on the rails, after saying, "Maybe we could do the same for you," we softly mention:

"To help me understand if we can do that or not,
would you mind if I asked a few questions?"

Why softly? We need to be unthreatening, almost tangential and matter-of-fact in our delivery.

We also specifically say "a few questions." In fact, we may ask quite a large number of questions to fully understand the client's situation. If the client thinks we are going to drill them with endless queries, they may become reluctant to cooperate. Once we get into it, though, and we start to help them better understand their own problems, they are appreciative rather than resentful.

The asking of the questions can be intrusive, quite interrogative, but it must never feel like an interrogation. We are here to help—"we come in peace"—and we must communicate this.

Presented in this fashion, you will be granted the opportunity to ask your questions. When the client agrees, you are now free to explore in detail their current situation, what they aspire to, what is holding them back, and what success would mean to them personally.

What happens if it doesn't work? What do you do if you don't get permission to ask your questions? The sad reality is that you will have little chance of convincing the client that you can help them solve their problems. It's time to politely down your insipid, bitter, cheap, lukewarm green tea, leave them as soon as possible, and find a better prospect.

Sometimes they are less direct, but equally evasive about answering questions. We do it ourselves when we are shopping, don't we? The store clerk asks us if there is anything we are looking for. What do we say? "Oh nothing, just browsing." Why do we say that?

We all love to buy, but we hate to be sold to. We know if we give the clerk any information, we are likely going to get into a sales conversation. We are not ready to give them our money, so we tell them something else to get rid of them. Clients do that to us, too. They withhold the pain points to get rid of us in a subtle manner that removes any hint of confrontation. This is particularly the case in Japan, where confrontation and directness are socially unacceptable. Here is another sales mantra for you:

> **❝**
>
> *Whenever I hit a wall of buyer non-cooperation, I don't waste my time. Instead, I go find someone who will tell me what their business needs are and whom I can properly serve.*
>
> **❞**

Amazingly, most of the salespeople who I meet as a buyer don't ask me any questions, but just blab on about the features of their product. They are untrained, and it shows. I met a senior Japanese guy, in his late fifties, who spoke to me about taking part in an HR Trade Show. It wasn't a cheap exercise for me, by the way. We spoke in Japanese and—for the next 40 minutes—he spoke like a machine gun, without once asking a single question.

He finally ran out of features to tell me about and just dribbled to a stop. I didn't say anything, because I was still wondering if a question would ever emerge from his lips. An uncomfortable silence ensued. To release the tension, he finally blurted out, "What do you think?"

I was reflecting on the fact that here we have a guy who has been in business in Japan for the better part of 30 years, and he is still clueless. What a waste of his golden youth, what an opportunity cost he has been to the companies for which he has worked. The perfect graduate example of underperforming OJT sales training!

I had a sales presentation given to me here in Tokyo by the sales director of a software vendor, and after some initial bromide-heavy pleasantries, he plunged straight into walking me through his slide presentation about the functionality of his solution. Not one question about my situation, my needs, my business, or my difficulties. Nothing. Amazing. He was an experienced guy in his forties, who had always been in sales! I didn't buy.

There were about two slides in that whole presentation that were relevant to me, but he used up most of our time on the inconsequential. What if he had been able to pinpoint what I needed early on and then focus the discussion on that instead? Come on! As salespeople, we must all do a lot better than this. If you know what you are doing, it is not that hard!

So, putting it all together, the Credibility Statement sequence flow for our business could run like this:

"Dale Carnegie Training helps to deliver the mind-set and behaviour changes needed in the team to produce improved results.

"An example of this was where we helped a very high-end retailer train their entire sales staff. They were getting nowhere, and now they are reporting to us that they are enjoying a 30% increase in sales.

"Maybe we could do the same for you? To help me understand if we can do that, would you mind if I asked a few questions?"

Now, obviously, this is for training in the service industry, and your product or service will be different. The formula, though, is universal; so the next task is to design the equivalent structure for your own business:

1. Your general capability
2. Your specific evidence of success
3. Your suggestion that you may be able to serve the client
4. Your permission request to transition to questions

This Credibility Statement should be short (under 30 seconds), delivered fluently and confidently (no *etoo*s, *anoo*s, uhms, or ahs). I said it is not so hard, but counterintuitively this takes a lot of preparation and practice, because it is so short. I should clarify that it is not difficult if you prepare properly. Every word is vital in the design stage, and we must deliver it perfectly and naturally.

It can also be repurposed as an ideal "elevator pitch" for those occasions when we must briefly explain what we do. This might be face-to-face at a networking function, by email, or over the phone.

If it is over the phone, then we would drop the request for permission to ask questions and replace it with: "Are you available next Tuesday, or is Thursday better?"

Warning!
Unless your product is specifically suited
to being sold in that way,
don't sell solutions over the phone.

Instead, secure a day and a time to meet. That is all we should be aiming for: the appointment.

You would think that, with all the literature available on selling, this would be common sense and common practice; but still salespeople try to sell the solution over the phone. The strike rate over the phone is extremely low for complex products or services, so stop beating yourself up and go for a time slot in their calendar instead.

Here in Tokyo, our clients in the pharmaceuticals industry note that hospitals restrict all salespeople to just one day a week to see the doctor. "See" being the operative word, because they only get one minute of the doctor's time! Like many large pharma companies, these clients had their own sales process, but they didn't have a Credibility Statement method.

Using our Dale Carnegie sales system, I introduced some Credibility Statement strategies for dealing with that nanosecond window, and they are bound to do much better. It is too early to declare "mission accomplished," and I will be interested to see how they execute these ideas.

If you only have such microscopic access to the buyer—like these pharmaceuticals salespeople do with busy doctors—you had better be saying something that has a hook big enough to land a great white shark.

An example of such a hook, in this case, might be a brief conversation which goes:

"Litigation lawyers are having a field day in the medical field in the United States, and we are all noticing this same trend coming to Japan. If you have 15 minutes later this week, I can show you some data on the Japan-approved list of drugs that are also being recommended by doctors in the US that have had zero or very low cases of claims. Can we get together to take a look? Would Thursday suit you or how about Friday?"

Let's break down the structure:

1. Doctors in Japan are scared about the increased frequency of claims against them by patients.
2. They are worried about rising costs associated with professional insurance, court cases, and legal fees.

3. By amplifying a conversation already going on in the doctor's mind, we have grabbed their attention.
4. The promise of useful data, which may save them having to deal with future trouble, is appealing.
5. Fifteen minutes does not seem an unreasonable time burden, despite their busy schedules.

If the hook is carefully crafted, then the client will prioritise time for you because you are providing something of differentiated value. Your competitors will be just bowing and saying "*yoroshiku onegaishimasu*," a vague but multi-use Japanese phrase that, in this context, means "let me know if I can help you with anything"—without actually offering anything concrete, beyond a cheesy smile.

The driving objective of sales is to solve clients' problems. We need to establish the client relationship based on a professional and competent first impression. The Credibility Statement does just that, and opens the door to permission to find the issues, offer solutions, and serve as a trusted business partner.

An alternative approach to the Credibility Statement is to use the Agenda Statement. This can be written down and sent ahead of time by email, presented at the meeting, or just spoken during the meeting.

We put together a meeting agenda, and it will start with a re-iteration of why this meeting is in the best interest of the customer.

It will then list the key agenda items, such as:

*   Some background on you and your firm
*   The client's current business situation
*   Where the client would like the business to be
*   Obstacles slowing the client down or preventing them from getting to where they want to be
*   What success would mean for the client personally

Following this explanation of the agenda, we then ask the client if they have any items they would like to add. This is an important step to help them feel part of the creation process and not just someone being bossed around by a pushy salesperson.

Their agreement on the agenda automatically includes their permission for us to ask questions.

Some buyers are very detail-oriented and want this level of structure. If you are selling in English and they are Japanese-speaking buyers, having something written down on paper in straightforward English helps the mutual communication go smoothly.

It might look like this:

Today's Meeting Agenda

Meeting Purpose

To explore opportunities to boost XYZ Company's business performance through the sharing of ideas and insights gained in the market

Discussion Items

1. Brief introduction of Dale Carnegie Training Japan and myself
2. XYZ's current business situation
3. XYZ's desired business performance
4. Barriers to business growth
5. What success would look like for XYZ
6. Additional items

This agenda simply captures the main points we need to uncover, to determine if we can actually help XYZ Company. The key point is to get permission to follow the agenda, which covers all the key areas we want to ask questions about.

ACTION STEPS

1. Craft your Credibility and Agenda Statements very stringently. Each word is like gold and should be treated as such.
2. Practice the delivery over and over, so that it is confident and smooth without sounding canned.
3. Always request permission to ask questions before you say one word about your solution line-up.

In the next chapter, we will learn some time-tested human relations principles that will improve our ability to become liked and trusted by buyers.

5—Salespeople Should Be Principled

In 1936, an unknown author, despite many frustrating years of writing and rejections, finally managed to get his manuscript taken up by a major publishing house. This work, *How to Win Friends and Influence People*, became a classic in the pantheon of self-help books—particularly those focused on how to be great with others. Surprisingly, many people in sales have never read it.

Plato, Socrates, Marcus Aurelius, and others were sharing thoughts substantially prior to 1936, and we still plumb their insights. Dale Carnegie has definitely joined that circle of established thinkers, offering wisdom and valuable ideas. His aim was to help all of us be better with each other, particularly in a business context. He did this by laying down some proven principles that can make us more successful in dealing with others, especially those not like us.

Salespeople should definitely be friendly, and must be successful with all personality types—not just people who are like them. Here are nine principles for helping us all become trusted by our clients.

1. Become genuinely interested in other people

Our buyers are actually more interested in what we know about what they want than in what we know about our product or service. It is a common mistake, though, to be so wrapped up in the features of our offering that we lose focus on the person buying it, and what they want.

At the extreme, transactional thinking means you don't care about the individual; you only care about their money. I wouldn't choose that road if I were you!

For a long career, we had better get busy really understanding our clients. The keyword in this principle is "genuine." Having a correct *kokorogamae*—or true intention—means we will be honestly focused on understanding the client, so that we can really serve them and build a partnership. We must be fully focused on their success, because wrapped up inside that outcome is our own success.

2. Talk in terms of the other person's interests

Salespeople have a nasty habit of selective listening and selective conversation around what they want to talk about. Their *kokoro-gamae* is centred on their interests, and the buyer's interests are secondary. Sales talk is a misnomer; there is no sales talk. There are well-designed questions and there are carefully crafted explanations of solution delivery that are tightly tied to what the buyer is interested in. Asking intelligent questions will uncover interests, and we need to do it with laser focus.

Sounds simple; but salespeople love to talk. They love the sound of their own voice and they become deaf to the client, often without even realising it. Check yourself during your next client conversation. Imagine a transcript of your words. Would they be 100% addressed to the buyer's interests. If not, then stop blathering and start talking in terms of their interests. By the way, Japanese buyers are rarely uncomfortable with silence, so don't feel pressured to fill the conversation gaps with pap while waiting for their response to your questions!

3. Be a good listener and encourage the other person to talk about themselves

Good listening means listening for what is not being said, as well as what we are hearing. It means not pretending to be listening while secretly thinking of our soon-to-be-unveiled brilliant response. It means not getting sidetracked by a single piece of key information, but taking in the whole of what is being conveyed. It means listening with our eyes—reading the body language and checking it against the words being offered.

Talkative salespeople miss so much key client information and then scratch their heads as to why they can't be more successful in selling. The client doesn't have the handbook indicating the flow of the sales process, where the questioning sequences are nicely aligned and arranged for maximum efficiency. Instead, the client conversation wanders all over the place, lurching from one topic to another, without any compunction.

I am just like that as a buyer. I have so many interests and will happily digress on the digressions of the digressions! Well-designed questions from the salesperson keep the whole thing on track and allow the client to speak about themselves at length. In those offerings from the buyer, we learn so much about their values, interests, absolute must-haves, desirables, primary interests, and dominant buying motives.

Japanese buyers usually need a considerable level of trust to be developed before they open up and talk about themselves. Japanese buyers also like to engage in small talk at the start. They do this to get an impression of us through what we say and how we say it. The typical Western approach is to get straight down to the business at hand. Don't go there. Have some questions of your own ready to go. These might include:

- *How long have you been working for this company?*
- *Is Tokyo your hometown?*
- *Where did you study English? It is very good!*

By the way, if they ask you what may be considered rather personal questions, don't be offended. They don't really care, they are just making light conversation.

It is exceedingly rare to wrap up an agreement in Japan with just one meeting. So, salespeople, play the long game and don't be in a rush. We are limbering up for a marathon, not a sprint.

4. Arouse in the other person an eager want

This is not huckster, carnival barker manipulation. This is becoming a great communicator, someone who can arouse passion and enthusiasm in others. Sales is the transfer of enthusiasm, based on the salesperson's belief in the "righteousness" of doing good, through supplying offerings that really help the buyer and their business.

One of the biggest barriers to success in sales is client inertia. They keep doing what they have always done—in the same way—

and keep getting the same result. Our job is to shake up that equation and help them get a better result through doing something new—buying our product or service.

We have to help them overcome their fears and persuade them to take action. In Japan, there is a penalty for action if something fails and less of a penalty associated with inaction, so the bias here is to do nothing.

Having a need and taking immediate action are not connected in the client's mind—not until we connect them. We have to fully explain the opportunity cost of no decision, no action, or no response to our proposal.

We achieve all of this by using well-thought-out questions that lead the buyer to draw the same conclusion that we have come to: that our offering is what they need, and that they need it right now.

This Socratic method of asking questions works because it helps to clarify the buyer's own thinking. Most salespeople don't ask enough questions because they are too busy talking about the features of their widget. We can arouse an eager want if we frame the questions well.

5. Let the other person feel that the idea is his or hers

Telling is not selling. Ramming our proposal down the client's throat is not selling. Being bombastic and dogged is not selling. Naturally, we will always have more information, data, and knowledge about our solution than the client. Blabbing on about the fine details won't persuade the client to buy.

Often, Japanese buyers expect a sales "lecture" on the proposal, so they can slip into the role of the critic. Avoid that scenario at all costs. All you will get out of that type of meeting is cheap, bitter green tea, and little more. Instead, go and find some buyers who will accept your questions.

Remember, we all own the world we help create. Our job is to help the client create a world we can share, that they feel deeply connected to, and about which they feel some ownership.

If I tell you some worthy insight, I still own it. If I ask questions that spur your thinking and help you gather some of those "lightbulb" moments, then you own that insight. We are always more likely to execute our own ideas than other people's suggestions.

Sales is about assisting clients in seeing possibilities they haven't considered. We have probably all had the experience when shopping of the store clerk's explanation alerting us to something we hadn't considered. This immediately framed our subsequent approach to that purchase. This is the job of the salesperson: to help the client reframe their worldview with rich and valuable insights that lead them to make the best buying decision—with us!

6. Try honestly to see things from the other person's point of view
Who we are today is built on a firm foundation of mistakes, errors of judgment, inexperience, and ineptitude. None of us were born perfect. We had to fail in order to learn what not to do, as well as what to do. We were not brilliant with new tasks from the start. We had to spend time to master the new and unfamiliar. In the beginning, we were clumsy until we gained some solid skills.

In other words, we are all hauling around prejudices, biases, painful memories, and firm views of the world—all built on a foundation of hard-won experiences. Salespeople trying to inject their views into this construct will feel like they are trying to penetrate a block of marble. In the original Greek and Latin, "education" meant "to lead out"—not "cram in"—information and ideas. We should embrace the classics and, like Michelangelo, draw the hidden David out of the marble.

To be successful in doing this, our communication skills must have empathy, so that we can get really deep with the client's worldview and experiences. We need to understand the creation platforms of their concepts, which reveal who they are today.

Let's get to know them at a more substantial level, so that we really get where they are coming from and, more importantly, understand their WHY. Most Japanese buyers are not all that open to being frank about what they want. Getting the WHAT or the HOW from a Japanese buyer, though, is much easier than getting the WHY. To get there, we need to build trust through multiple meetings, have big dabs of patience, and have a correct *kokorogamae* or true intention.

This requires that we stop concentrating on ourselves and what we want. Instead, focus on the buyer's needs. We must suspend our own surety of our concept's creation platform and see things afresh, in an open, unbiased way. When we can get that clarity, the words coming out of our mouths will be perfectly aligned with what resonates most deeply with the client's needs, and they will buy our offerings.

7. Get the other person saying, "yes, yes," immediately

"Yes momentum" is an old idea in sales. It works on the psychological principle that a series of positive responses will lead to an acceptance of our offer. A simplistic understanding of this idea would see our hearty sales hero designing a long set of killer questions, the only logical response to which is a robotic affirmative.

For example: "If you were able to reduce costs, would this be of help to your business?" Everyone wants to save costs in business, so the only logical answer is yes. The problem with this type of approach is that it becomes manipulative, as the salesperson belts out a whole series of these can-only-be-answered-by-yes questions.

It reminds me of those nodding animal figures that bob up and down in the back of cars. Expecting to fast-track your way into a sale through this client head-bobbing is a misunderstanding of the principle.

The principle is saying let's get "yes, yes" responses immediately, but not exclusively. In Japanese, *hai* means "yes," but this is the yes of "I hear you," not the yes of "I agree with you." We need to understand this and ask the question in a way that differentiates between the two responses.

We will want to design some "closed questions" that help the buyer clarify their thinking about our proposition. A closed question is one to which only a "yes" or "no" answer is possible. We should start with one or two "yes" questions that narrow the focus to a positive investigation of the value of our solution, when judged against the alternatives. It should not become a "Yesfest" though.

After getting some positive responses, we should begin asking the WHY behind the responses. This helps us dig deeper into the drivers of an affirmative decision.

Clients, as mentioned, will wander all over the prairie once they get going, so we have to shepherd them back on topic. A good way to do that is to ask a closed question to which they can easily answer "yes."

Now we can keep the conversation moving in the right direction, without the whole process becoming artificial and manipulative. "Yes momentum" is good, but best in moderation.

8. Be sympathetic with the other person's ideas and desires

Understanding the dominant motive of the buyer is the Holy Grail of sales. Of course, we need to know the primary buying motive—the WHAT—but to really serve the client we need to know the WHY. In particular, how will this buying decision advance their career or their business? Where can we fit in, to become a booster of their success?

Risk aversion is a strong emotion in all of us—especially among Japanese buyers. We have all been burnt at some stage through a purchase that failed to satisfy, and which we immediately regretted. We paid too much, or it broke straight away, and the salesperson's spiffy spiel wasn't matched by the product's performance.

Some people have an MBA, but we all have an MDS: a Master's Degree in Scepticism. Japanese buyers, by the way, all seem to have a PhD in Scepticism of Salespeople—especially foreign salespeople.

As salespeople, we need to be mindful of the client's emotions and find ways to legitimately prove our solution will not disappoint. The client's desire is to improve or defend their situation. No one wishes to go backwards in business.

Clients have their own ideas about how that is best done, and our job is to find out WHAT it is and WHY they think so. We may have reached a different conclusion on the HOW, but by understanding what is driving them we can more easily explain where our solution gels with what they want to achieve. We can succeed by getting them to do most of the talking and by prompting new thoughts through great questions.

9. Dramatise your ideas

When we pick up the phone to speak with our client, or when we sit down in the meeting room with them, they are bursting at the seams with "stuff" in their heads. They are wrestling with what happened yesterday, what they have to get through today, and worrying about what will happen tomorrow.

These days, we are all having much more face-to-device time than face-to-face time. There is no downtime anymore, as we slip out our phone to check everything we ever wanted to know—and lots of things we don't need to know. Salespeople are competing with this internal and external noise for client brain space.

We need to be primed to break through the clutter and grab the client's attention. Otherwise, we will never be able to sell our wares. We need to be working out how our client likes to communicate. Are they micro- or macro-focused? Are they interested in people or task outcomes?

Once we have established the form of communication that best resonates with them, we should be looking for various ways to dramatise our recommendations.

Vocal word-picture drawing is a great skill for a salesperson, as we choose evocative words that our listener can see in their mind's eye. To register the greatest reaction with the buyer, collect "power words" that you can pepper your sales explanation with.

We need to become great storytellers, with lots of "colour and movement," to grab their nanosecond attention spans.

In regards to delivery, it may vary quite a bit. We may be very direct or we may be very thoughtful in our expression, in accordance with the client's preferred style of communication.

We are giving them the floor for the bulk of the meeting, and thus have only a limited window for our words; so we need to be very deliberate in what we are going to say. Lengthy blarney is a thing of the past—you simply don't have enough airtime to blab on anymore. We need word injection precision when we speak.

The words themselves, and the vocal range we use to articulate them, are all important. We need to use speed—fast and slow—for emphasis. Put the power in for some words and take the power out entirely for others.

Word emphasis can completely change the meaning of a sentence.

Try this: "I didn't say he hit his friend."

Repeat the sentence seven times out aloud, emphasising the word in capitals.

1. *I* didn't say he hit his friend.
2. I *DIDN'T* say he hit his friend.
3. I didn't *SAY* he hit his friend.
4. I didn't say *HE* hit his friend.
5. I didn't say he *HIT* his friend.
6. I didn't say he hit *HIS* friend.
7. I didn't say he hit his *FRIEND*.

By emphasising a particular word, the inference of the sentence is changed.

This simple exercise underlines that we have a powerful tool at our disposal: our voice. We also need facial expressions and gestures that are congruent with what we are saying. These add strength to amplify the key message.

Dale Carnegie was a leader in thinking about being excellent with people. His principles are universal and timeless. We are in sales and we can adopt these principles to become more effective in dealing with our buyers.

ACTION STEPS
1. Read or reread *How to Win Friends and Influence People*.
2. Make these principles your mantra for building good relations with people.
3. Apply these principles in every sales conversation with clients.

In the next chapter, we will show how to provide unprecedented value to the buyer.

6—Let's Go for the Sales Bull's-eye

Sales solutions are what make the business world thrive. The client has a problem, and we fix it. Our goods or services are delivered, outcomes are achieved, and everybody wins. In a lot of cases, however, these are only partial wins. Problems and issues are a bit like icebergs—there is a lot more going on below the surface than a ship's captain can spot from the bridge. The salesperson's role is to go after the whole iceberg, not just the obvious bit floating above the waterline.

The standard sales interview is based on two models comprising the outer circles that surround a bull's-eye. The extreme periphery is the "telling is selling" model. This ensures that the salesperson does most of the talking. The client is subjected to a constant bombardment of features until they either buy, die, or retreat. The second model, the inner circle adjoining the bull's-eye, is the solution model of providing outcomes that best serve the client, based on what they understand to be their problem.

The latter is a much better tool, and is in pristine condition because so few salespeople use it. Rapidly firing features at the client rarely provides success because of the randomness of the proffering of alternatives. Welcome to the "toss enough mud at the wall and some is bound to stick" school of sales. Aligning the problem fix with the client need in the solution model is the mark of the semi-professional. There is nothing wrong with this model, but what are the rock star sales masters doing?

They are zipping up their wetsuits and diving into the icy water under the problems-and-issues iceberg, inspecting things closely and really understanding the full scope of the situation. They are on a mission to find what nobody else is seeing. Their ability to deliver unseen and unconsidered insights is pure gold for clients.

Mentally picture our big red bull's-eye at the centre of a series of concentric circles. Stating the features of a product or service is the first level, the very outer circle. The next inner circle contains our solutions constructed around what the client already knows.

The highest level is suggesting solutions for problems that the client isn't even aware of yet.

Truly magical client reactions would be: "Oh, I hadn't thought of that" or "We haven't allowed for that!" Think about your own experience. Any time you have been a buyer and have uttered those words to yourself—as a result of insight from the salesperson—have you experienced a major breakthrough in your world view? Now that is the bull's-eye we want right there. Is it easy? Of course not, but this is what separates the sales greats from the hoi polloi.

The salesperson who can provide that type of perspective, alerting clients to over-the-horizon issues, provides such value that they quickly become the client's trusted business partner. Be it in archery or business, hitting the bull's-eye is no walk in the park. Insight can't be plucked from the air at will. Plumbing one's experiences, sorting and sifting for corresponding relevancies, and then diving deeply into the client's world looking for alignment are the skills required.

In a way, our ignorance of the intimate particulars of the client's business is an advantage. Paraphrasing famed management consultant and author Peter Drucker, our success can come by asking a lot of "stupid" questions. A salesperson has an outside perspective, untainted and pure. There is no inner veil obscuring the view, no preconceived notions or ironclad assumptions clouding judgment.

Counterintuitively, the fact that we don't know what we don't know becomes our strength. Ignorance allows us to question orthodoxy in a way that insiders can't, because of inertia, groupthink, company culture, or the internal politics of the organisation.

When salespeople serve numerous clients—be it in the same industry or across industries—they pick up vital strategic and tactical commercial intelligence. Researching various clients' problems, experiences, triumphs, and disasters is valuable—but only if you know how to process the detail.

In all our companies, we can only see clearly what we are doing ourselves. We all exemplify that Japanese saying: "The frog in the well does not know the ocean." Everything is too familiar, and so we don't question everyday normality. We don't have the opportunity to peak behind the curtain and look into what our competitors are doing.

It is also very rare for company personnel to do study tours of totally unrelated businesses. If we classified industries alphabetically, in a standard business setting, representatives from A and Z would rarely meet, let alone get to trade ideas and experiences. Salespeople, however, are floating around businesses and therefore are able to know many different wells and oceans. Processing information in this data-saturated world is how the gold is found. The ability to select and apply one particularly successful thing in a different context is a commercially valuable skill.

How can salespeople get that skill? One way in which salespeople can provide over-the-horizon value is by being highly observant. Take what you have seen working elsewhere for one client—in a different company or industry—and apply it for your current client. Sounds rather easy, doesn't it? The reality is that pressured salespeople miss much, record little, remember less, and blag their way through most of their client meetings. Let's all slow down, listen, think, and then innovate. The answers are often right there, but we miss out because we are too busy. We are unaware, and therefore aren't looking in the right places.

Another way to get that skill is to do practical research. Based on what you already know, build up a point of view on an industry and check it against what your clients are telling you (or conduct company surveys). Delve into nascent potential problems, arrive at your hypothesis, and be the first mover. The real-time insight garnered from this type of activity allows salespeople to become rock stars in the business world. They are providing "take it to the bank" added value for the buyer.

We won't always be able to conjure up a bull's-eye. However, in trying to do so, our aspirations, general direction, and thinking will be correct. Our *kokorogamae*, or true intention, will be on track. By comparison, our competitors will lag well behind, still waffling on about features or playing detective interrogating clients. We have to move on to a higher dimension, where clients seek us out. They do so because they recognise the value of what we offer. In sales, the inner-most circle—the big red bull's-eye—leads straight to the winner's circle, and that is where we must be. Let's make "insight" our springboard to success.

ACTION STEPS

1. Look for questions the client hasn't even thought of yet.
2. Create a point of view on an industry and test this against your client's reality.
3. Look for areas where you can introduce a solution successfully applied in another context.
4. Lead with insight.

In the next chapter, let's look at how to build trust.

7—How to Be Likeable and Trustworthy in Sales

I know I am not a patient man, but it has always frustrated me how hopeless some salespeople are in Japan. It doesn't have to be so bad. Over the past 25 years, I have been through thousands of job interviews with salespeople. We also teach sales for our clients' teams and so, as a training company, we see the good, the bad, and the ugly—a very broad gamut of salespeople. We are a buyer of services and products ourselves, and so are actively on the receiving end of the sales process. Well, actually, that is a blatant exaggeration. There are so few salespeople operating in Japan using a sales process, but there are millions of them out there just winging it (badly).

Why? OJT is the main pedagogical system in Japan for training the new salesperson. This works well if your boss has a clue and knows about selling. Sadly, there are few leaders like that populating Japan's sales landscape. So what you get are hand-me-down "techniques" that are ineffective. Even worse, these techniques are poorly executed in the hands of newbies. The bosses can't add much value because they were taught the same way.

We like to buy, but few of us want to be sold to. We want to do business with people we like and trust. We will do business with people we don't like and—very, very rarely—with people we don't trust. Neither is our preference though.

The million-dollar question is: "What makes YOU, the salesperson, likeable and trustworthy?"

THE FIRST FEW SECONDS DECIDES IT ALL

Building rapport in the first meeting with a prospective client is a critical make-or-break opportunity for establishing likability or trust. When you think about it, this is just the same as in a sales job interview. In both cases, we enter an unfamiliar environment and greet strangers who are brimming over with preoccupation, doubt, uncertainty, reluctance, and scepticism. If a salesperson can't handle a job interview and build rapport straight away, then it is unlikely they are doing much better out in the field, regardless of their glowing rock star resume.

As I mentioned, over the past 25 years I have interviewed more than 3,000 salespeople for jobs. You might be thinking that is quite a large number for one guy to get through. It is. What we find in Japan is that there are very few people who know how to write a proper job resume. You either get the guy flipping hamburgers telling you he ran NASA, or the gal actually running NASA who comes across like the graveyard shift worker at McDonald's. The end result is that you wind up interviewing way more people than normal.

The world of business is moving faster and faster. Consequently, we are making up our minds very quickly when we meet someone. So what must we do to build trust in those vital first few seconds? Strangely, we need to pay more attention to our posture!

Huh?

It is common sense really; standing up straight communicates confidence and personal power. Also, in Japan, bowing from a half leaning forward posture, especially while we are still on the move, makes us look weak, uncertain, and unconvincing. Maybe Japanese companies are fine with this as a cultural norm around humility, but it is a red flag for those hiring for *gaishikei* (multinational) companies.

So, aspirant interviewees and hard-working salespeople, walk in to the meeting, stand straight and tall, make eye contact, hold it, stop, and then bow or shake hands depending on the circumstances. Smiling at the same time may also be good, depending on the situation.

Why is smiling not obligatory? Japanese people are much more formal than most Westerners (especially my fellow laid-back Australians), and being *majime* (serious) is considered a wonderful thing. The difficulty I have always had with that *majime* number is figuring out the difference between a serious face and an angry face. They tend to look exactly the same to me. If your host is very doughty and serious, hold off on the smile offensive until the atmosphere warms up a bit.

If there is a handshake involved, then, at least when dealing with foreigners, Japanese colleagues please drop the dead-fish grasp or the double-hander (gripping the forearm or the elbow with the other hand). The latter is the classic "insincere politician double hand-grip." Not a winning first impression there!

Some Japanese businesspeople I have met have become overly Westernised, in that they apply a bone-crusher grip when shaking hands. I have even met some petite Japanese business-women who apply massive grip strength when shaking hands as they try to out man the men. Ladies, chill on the power handshake. It sounds like very basic advice, but please, Japanese salespeople, learn how to shake hands properly.

It cuts the other way, too. When we foreigners shake hands with Japanese counterparts, we should be introducing the right amount of grip pressure to convey reliability rather than total world domination.

Too weak or too strong are unforced errors that impinge on building the all-important first impression.

Bowing is another area where foreigners must be careful. You might recall that US President Barack Obama gave a very, very deep ninety-degree bow to the Emperor. Nobody in Japan com-plained about the depth of the bow, but it was a bit too deep. In business, trying to outdo the locals is faintly ridiculous. So unless you are meeting the Emperor, I would keep the bow respectful; and a thirty-degree angle will suffice.

By the way, we probably only have a maximum of 7–10 sec-onds to get that first impression correct, so every second counts. Why so short? Clients are quick to make snap judgments today. As salespeople we just can't afford to leave anything to chance.

This is an important start to the conversation, so let me clari-fy the steps. When you first see the client, make eye contact. I don't mean burn a hole in the recipient's head, but hold eye contact at the start for around six seconds and, if appropriate, smile.

This eye contact/smile combination conveys consideration, reliability, and confidence—all attributes we are looking for in our business partners. We combine this with the greeting and the usual pleasantries: "Thank you for seeing me" and "Thank you for your time today." Now, what comes next is very important.

We segue into establishing rapport through initial light conversation. Japan has some fairly unremarkable evergreens in this regard, usually talking about the weather, the distance you have travelled to get to the meeting, etc. These are okay, but let's try to do better than these garden-variety contributions. Try and differentiate yourself with something that is not anticipated or standard.

Also, be careful about complimenting a prominent feature of the lobby, office, or meeting room. I was in a beautiful, brand-new office in Tokyo and they have a really impressive moss wall in the lobby. I will guarantee that my hosts have heard obvious comments about the moss wall from every visitor who has preceded me. "Wow, what an impressive moss wall!" or "Wow, that is a spectacular entry feature!" Boring!

As salespeople, we need to do better than that and should be aiming to say something unexpected, intelligent, and memorable. In this case, perhaps, "Have you found that team motivation has lifted since you moved to this impressive new office?" or "Have you found that brand equity with your newish clients has improved since moving here?"

This gets the focus immediately off you, the salesperson, and on to the client and their business. For example, if you are a training company like us, you definitely want hints about how their team motivation is going, as you may have a solution for them. What would be some things you could lead with that will be relevant to your industry, sector, or business?

Having a good stock of conversation starters should be basic for every salesperson. It might mean imparting some startling information that they may not have heard. For example:

"I read recently that the number of young people in Japan aged 15–24 has halved over the last 20 years. Are you concerned about future talent retention as employee demand exceeds supply?"

We might educate the client with some industry information they may not be aware of, but which would be deemed valuable. Take that opportunity and supply some useful insight or information to get the client thinking about a problem or issue they may not have given enough attention to yet.

An example for us would be:

> *"Dale Carnegie's recent research into engagement amongst employees found there were three critical factors impacting motivation. The relationship with the immediate supervisor, the team's belief in the direction being set by senior management, and the degree of pride in the organisation. What are you seeing in your organisation around the area of engagement and motivation?"*

What information do you have access to that would allow you to lead with adding value to the client's business?

We face a lot of competition for the brain space of our prospective clients. Busy people have a lot on their mind, and we are an interruption in their day. Some of our prospective clients may be moving continuously from one meeting to another, so their attention span is shredded and the details begin to blur. They may have their eyes open, but their mind may not be in the room nor necessarily focused on you. To counteract that possible external preoccupation—and to get them back in the room with you—use a question.

By way of demonstration, if I suddenly asked you, "What month were you born in?", I guarantee I will have your 100% attention. Questions are powerful disrupters of preoccupation, and we should have a stock of little beauties that we can wheel out when needed. For example:

> *"Most people I talk to say the government's new economic policies are not having any significant impact on their business so far. Have you seen any benefits yet?"*

Another might be:

"My clients' opinions seem to have changed—they are becoming more concerned about possible further increase in taxes. Is that an issue for your company?"

How about:

"The yen is really becoming quite volatile. Does that have any significant impact on your business?"

We want them talking about their business, because this is going to provide us with insights for a later line of questioning, as we try to uncover their performance gaps, needs, aspirations, and requirements.

As flagged, the very first seconds of meeting someone are vital to building the right start to the business relationship. In modern commerce, we are all so judgmental and quick to make assumptions.

Dressing the wrong way may even disqualify us before we get to open our mouths. By the way, in Japan, with some rare exceptions, you can rarely make a mistake by being on the more formal, rather than the casual, side in personal presentation.

Simple initial errors in posture, greeting, and conversation can be our undoing. Let's get our sales basics right and make sure we totally nail that first impression. This is the rapport building stage of the sales process, and it is both a science and an art we need to perfect.

ACTION STEPS

1. Refine an image through dress, posture, and eye contact that projects confidence.
2. Stock your opening comments such that they are really well differentiated from all of your competitors, who have swanned in ahead of you and who distinguished themselves by making the most banal observations.
3. Provide useful business references to introduce something new to the client that gets the attention off you and on to the client's business.

In the next chapter, we will look at the ups and down of prospecting activity and its impact on revenue.

8—The Death Valley of Sales

S ales cannot run like a manufacturing production line. We are not making industrial cheese here. This is more like an artisanal pursuit, sometimes closer to art than science. Yet, every sales force on the planet has targets which are usually uniform. Each month, the sales team has to deliver a specified amount of revenue, rolling up into a predetermined annual target. The construct may be logical, but sales is far from logical, as it is steeped in emotion, luck, and magic.

Having said that, sales is also a numbers game, and to some extent pseudoscientific. There are accepted algorithms that apply:

1. You call a certain number of people
2. Speak to a lesser number
3. Meet a few
4. From that residual group, you conclude an agreement

There are ratios, which, when calculated over time, apply as averages linking activity with results. So we:

1. Call 100 people
2. Speak to 80
3. See 20
4. Strike a deal with 5

In this construct, to make one sale we need to call 20 people on average.

With this type of precision available, you would think that we could industrialise the sales process and confidently set annual targets, neatly divided into units of 12, to arrive at a consistent stream of revenue achievement. As the sales team obligingly tracks to the revenue plan, sales managers would be multitasking, sipping their afternoon martinis, propping up their cowboy boots on the desk, and carefully calculating their next car upgrade.

Sadly, it doesn't work like this. Sales flow without rhyme or reason, some months exceeding the target and other months missing it completely. Some salespeople are precociously consistent producers while others are annoyingly unpredictable; and some are just annoying because they don't seem to be doing much. Why is there this perplexing inability to automate the production of results? The Death Valley of Sales is the problem.

This is the plunge between sales peaks. It is the lull in the fighting, the quiet before the storm, the brief interlude in the phony war of sales. Salespeople work hard, usually because they are on commission structures that guarantee not very much if they don't produce.

Japan is a little different. Basically, there is either a base and commission or straight salary and bonuses system. Few salespeople in Japan are on 100% commission. Why? Because they don't have to be and the Japanese preference for risk aversion means forget it! Nevertheless, they know they have to produce, so they tend to be diligent.

Commission structures vary, but many "industrial structures" specify that you have to hit a monthly or quarterly target before your commission kicks in. If this is too industrial, it may fail to take into account seasonal downturns, because each target unit tends to be the same throughout the year. This is hardly motivating, and probably needs a bit more nuance around expectations and reality.

Salespeople cannot be consistently successful unless they have two great professional skills. They must be machine-like time managers and they must be highly disciplined. The two interlock. The ebb and flow of sales is based on customer activity. Networking, cold calling, following up with previous clients, chasing leads that come through marketing activities, etc., all takes considerable time.

If we pump out enough client contact activity, we will get appointments, sales, and therefore generate follow-up. Time starts to disappear through the mining activities that made us active in the first place. We can't do the prospecting work because we are too busy executing the follow-up. Once the fog of being busy clears, though, we suddenly see that we have a very pitiful pipeline ahead of us. So, we work like a demon again to kick-start new lead generation.

Downturns in activity lead to massive holes in revenue. This is the Death Valley of Sales. It is the messy counterpoint to industrial sales production, which is consistent, uniform, and—when graphed for boss presentations—beautifully shaped, balanced, and ascetically pleasing to upper management.

To avoid this valley phenomenon, we need to make time to keep prospecting every week—hence the requirement for excellent time management skills and the discipline to make sure we are doing it every week. Otherwise, we find our time for pipeline development is stolen away by client demands, emergencies, mistake correction, more detailed discussions, and results follow-up with the buyer.

Salespeople who do not block out time in their diary for prospecting every day will be Death Valley dwellers in short order. They will be joined there by those who don't plan their day in detail. That means planning the necessary activities with numbered action priorities. Winging it, being "spontaneous," and living in the moment unshackled from schedules are all delusional salespeople activities that cannot be part of a successful sales life.

If we don't wish to enter the Death Valley of Sales, we must block out time for prospecting and craft a carefully prioritised daily To Do list. Having crafted it, we must follow the work items in order of priority. Failure here is permanent, because the consistency of production will elude us forever. We will get lost in the harsh environment of the valley and perish by the wayside.

Let's commit to building the pipeline every day and avoid the Death Valley of Sales at all costs.

ACTION STEPS

1. Adjust sales team targets to account for seasonality of sales to keep their motivation high.
2. Know your sales activity ratios required to produce sales revenues.
3. Become a maniac about good time management and self-discipline.
4. Protect time in the schedule for doing prospecting each week.

In the next chapter, let's look at what we must do to improve our listening skills.

9—How to Be a Better Listener

There is a tremendous amount of noise buzzing around in the world of business today. The noisiest portion is the bit going on between our ears, inside our brains. We are so busy, so immersed in what we are doing, we are forgetting some of the basics.

The blue screen addiction we have all become hooked on means there is barely a minute of slow time anymore. We are texting, reading, surfing the net, jumping around all over the place. We are running our lives as a meeting conveyor belt, moving from one topic to the next, multitasking like demons on speed.

The upshot is that we are no longer really concentrating on what is happening around us, as we become totally self-absorbed. The skill of communication has become a one-dimensional activity—we are getting out what we want to say, but not really listening to what our client has to say. We go through the motions of pretending to listen, but we are only partially listening. Even worse, we are mainly specialising in selective listening. Seeking their words of agreement, we filter out delivery and all the hidden codes therein.

We are also very quick. We are second-guessing the conversation and rapidly forming our next intervention, well before the client has gotten to the point of the story. Significantly, the point of the story may not only be in the words. The delivery by the client has tremendous meaning, but if we are concentrating on what we will say next, we will be missing that part of the communication.

We are also pretty deadly when it comes to cutting off the client, as we believe we have cleverly guessed where they were headed—even if that is not the case. The central points of the sales process can easily get bogged down in some minor aside to the key points, because we have zeroed in on a minor element, imagining it is the key, when maybe it is not. If we become habitual interrupters, we may be breezing through life existing on half conversations, never really plumbing the depths of what others are trying to convey to us.

Reflecting on these observations, do you feel you are a good listener, a gold medal-winning listener? As we say in Japanese, can you *kuki wo yomu* (空気を読む)—read the atmosphere of the conversation—beyond the words being spoken? *Ku* here means empty, *ki* means spirit, and *yomu* means to read. We can interpret this expression as reading between the lines and understanding what is not being said. Japanese people all seem to believe they have well-developed skills in "reading the atmosphere." Therefore, stating the obvious is not necessary for them. Fine, except that it may not be obvious to you; so, you need to really listen to what is being said.

Do you feel you might need to improve your listening skills? Good listeners display a pattern of distinctive behaviours, and these can be easily practiced and mastered. Here are some simple ways to be better at the art of conversation by being a better listener.

1. Stay focused.
Minimise external distractions and pay close attention to what the client is saying. A classic example is the fact that we are often guilty of complaining that we can't remember the names of the potential clients we have just met at a networking event. Part of the reason is that we probably did not focus well enough to clearly catch the name in the first place.

Maybe we were distracted by what was going on around us. Maybe we were so busy thinking about what we wanted to say that we were tuning the client out. Maybe the potential client mumbled their name or fired it out like a bullet and we couldn't catch the sounds. If we can't even get their name right, we are at a big disadvantage. We need to really focus on the client and get their name right as a starting point of business discipline.

2. Be patient.
Staying focused also requires patience. Suspend the desire to say

something and just let the client speak. Everyone loves to talk, especially about themselves, so indulge them. Focus on them and they will appreciate it. Former US President Bill Clinton is renowned for his ability to charm the people he meets.

The common thread amongst those commenting on his charm is that he spoke to them in a way that made them feel as if they were the only person in the room. He would ask them a question and get them talking. The result was a feeling that they were having a one-on-one conversation with Bill, despite the noisy, crowded venue and the hordes of onlookers.

For that brief interlude, he was absorbed in their answer to the exclusion of all else. That is the type of focus we need to adopt when speaking with clients.

3. Interpret both words and emotions.
The words clients use are just one part of what they're saying. You can capture the whole message by also paying attention to the emotions behind the words.

Japan is particularly challenging in this regard. The suppression of emotions or the disguising of the real emotion is well entrenched in the culture, so it can be very hard to gauge what is really behind the words.

Foreigners sometimes complain that Japanese are "two-faced." They say this because they don't yet understand how the culture tolerates the subtle difference between *tatemae* (public truth) and *honne* (real truth).

This distilling of what is behind the words requires the full power of concentration on that client, as well as a total visual interrogation of every morsel of body language and voice inflection we can muster.

4. Do not interrupt.
Interruptions decrease effective communication. We assume that we are smarter than the person speaking, because we have superpowers that allow us to anticipate where the conversation is

headed, even before it gets there. Maybe we should be more humble and polite, and let them finish.

This type of attitude shows respect and courtesy—two commodities that are in rare supply these days. Another reason people interrupt is that they are nervous and can't control their emotions. This is a fatal flaw and says a lot of negative things about you, things that perhaps you don't want to broadcast to the entire business community.

5. Resist filtering.
Be open-minded; don't judge what someone says by your values only. Offence is often taken in error. We attach a certain interpretation to something said by the potential client that was never thought or intended. We react quickly, start arguing with the client, and tie ourselves into knots. We can get into lots of trouble because of this tendency.

6. Use humour carefully.
Pathetic attempts at humour or sardonic wit can also become socially combustible when they fall way short of the mark or the cultural differences are too great for the joke to be understood. Very few Japanese ever get the sardonic, ironic, self-flagellating style of humour, because the cultural context is missing or because the comedian is fundamentally hopeless in the first place.

Having spent 12 years here selling in the international trade arena, I noticed that my fellow Aussies were notorious for this use of incomprehensible humour, in a failed effort to lighten the atmosphere. Actually, it does work a charm, but it needs to be preceded by the consumption of large amounts of alcohol after business hours. During the day, it tends to bomb badly.

7. Summarise the message.
Be sure you've heard something correctly by offering a quick summary of what the client has said. This need not apply to all parts of a conversation or to every conversation, but when we are getting

down to it, this is the time to clearly indicate you have fully understood what you are being told.

The military worked this out a long time ago, and even though we don't have to adopt their jargon—"roger that"—we can adopt their basic idea of repeating the key information as a checking mechanism to eliminate future problems.

8. Wait your turn.
Try not to jump in too soon with your own opinion. Be sure to "wait your turn" to speak.

Japanese is a great language for teaching us to be patient and to wait for the punch line. In Japanese grammar, the verb comes at the end of the sentence; so as we are listening, we don't know if the statement is going to be positive or negative, past, present, or future. There's no point jumping in and cutting someone off when speaking in Japanese, because you have no clue where they are going with the story until the very end.

This is a good discipline to adopt for ourselves in general. If you are an ardent interrupter, an unreformed impatient, a spirited replier, a seasoned sentence-finisher, then ease up. Purse your lips together and let no sound emerge until the client has stopped. It may be killing you to wait, but your listening skills will skyrocket in proportion to your degree of patience.

The lost art of listening needs to make a comeback, and we need to be the poster children for the revolution. Let's get back to business basics and listen our way to great success.

ACTION STEPS
1. Stay focused
2. Suspend the desire to speak
3. Interpret both words and emotions
4. Do not interrupt
5. Resist filtering
6. Resist your pathetic attempts at humour
7. Summarise the message
8. Wait to express your own opinion

In the next chapter, we will work on how to prepare for our client meetings.

10—How to Prepare Properly for Client Meetings

We are all very busy, rushing around finding new clients, developing leads, networking, cold calling, attending client meetings, preparing proposals, and later executing the follow-through on what has been promised. Somewhere in this process, some key basics start to go missing. One of those basics is proper preparation for client meetings.

This is rather ironic, because we salespeople have never had it so good. In this modern age, so much information is just a few clicks away. Listed client companies very conveniently include their financial details, strategies, corporate officer information, etc. in annual reports on their websites.

Invariably, we will see a modern, besuited business Titan posing in the corporate corner office. In addition to the PR division's photographic efforts, there will be a substantial article or interview with the CEO, outlining the way forward for the company. The key organisational goals and milestones are on display for all to see.

A few minutes spent finding and reading this information will give the salesperson a very clear idea of the key business drivers for the company's strategy. The financial section will also tell us how the entity is tracking against its declared goals. It may even provide a breakdown at the divisional or country level, which is pure gold to someone about to meet a local decision-maker from that firm.

Being able to tie what you sell to the goals they have set for themselves instantly makes the context relevant and places the discussion on the right basis. Talking about your contribution to their ROI is of great interest to those who have responsibility to deliver the goals established by senior management. So rather than talking about what you want—to sell something—it is better to focus the discussion on how you can help them achieve their goals.

How many salespeople, though, bother to do this prior to calling on the client? Not enough! If we turn up at their office and say, "Tell me about your business," this speaks volumes about our lack of research on the company beforehand. It would be much better to ask a well-designed question that relates to the goals that have been set forth within that company. We should be looking for context whereby we can show how helpful we can be in solving their local issues, which are preventing them from satisfying their corporate goals.

We should be coming into that meeting talking about the most relevant issues facing the team we are visiting. We might say:

> *"I notice that your company president has made it a clear goal to grow the business by 12% next year. Given the current business climate, that sounds pretty tough. Is that also the commitment you need to deliver from the Japan business?"*

This is a great question because we have indicated that we have done our homework—we are aware of the firm's goals and are empathetic. We are also checking if the local business has the same issues. If they answer that the local unit must grow by 30%, it sets us up for a very interesting conversation about how they are going to achieve that, and why their local goal is so much larger.

We want to capture the scale of the gap between their current performance and their required performance, plus their chances of bridging that gap without our help. If we find out that the opportunity to grow 30% in Japan is a snap, because business conditions here are so much better than everywhere else for them, we may have a hard time showing where we can be helpful. Having a need is the first prerequisite. No need, no sale.

On the other hand, if they are really suffering from having such a large target, then perhaps we are the solution. If so, they will be all ears to hear how we can help. We could ask "How is business?" and they may or may not choose to enlighten us to their reality.

Remember, everyone loves to buy, but no one wants to be sold to. So, the less you have to tell a salesperson, the less likely you will be sold anything. If we are able to quickly lead the conversation into a deeper stage, we are more likely to find out if we have a new client here. This should be our goal, and we should be using the best resources available to achieve our goal.

Apart from the firm itself, there are also the individuals we will meet from the firm. They will probably have a presence on Google, Yahoo, Facebook, LinkedIn, Twitter, Instagram, YouTube, and other platforms. A quick search on their name will turn up useful background information, which may allow us to draw out some things we have in common. Maybe we both studied at the same university or previously worked in the same industry or lived in the same location (state or town) or have the same hobbies. These are speedy connectors between two total strangers.

In sales, we need our buyers to know, like, and trust us. The like and trust parts are the difficult bits—especially at the initial stages of the relationship. Sharing things in common is a great way to quickly establish credibility and a relationship.

Let's take my example. I am from Queensland, grew up in Brisbane, support the Brisbane Broncos rugby team, went to Griffith University, and practice karate. There is a wealth of speedy connectors right there. If you are trying to sell me something, here is the brilliant part: you can find out all of this online in about five minutes.

Start our meeting by commenting on how well Queensland has been doing in the Origin rugby, and you and I are off to a great start! It means you know about the rabid Queensland versus New South Wales State rivalry and how important it is to native Queenslanders like me to win.

I am a buyer of goods and services here in Japan. Over the past 25 years, not one salesperson has tried to connect with me and establish a relationship through some common connectors. Maybe 25 years ago that was probably difficult. These days, however, given what is out there now in the public domain, there is no excuse for salespeople calling on me (particularly over the past ten years) not to try to connect in this way.

It is the same for most people we meet. We can get the relationship off to a flying start if we bother to invest the time to find out their key details. Yes, we are all very busy; but that is not a sufficient excuse. This is a potential client, and they are hard enough to come by at any point. We salespeople are simply not doing a good enough job to use the tools at our command today.

It is crazy when you think about it. Trying to build a connection and establish a positive first impression must be every salesperson's goal when meeting new clients for the first time. You will create a first impression, one way or another. Just what type of first impression would you like to create? The more you know about the person you are meeting, the greater likelihood you can create a great first impression.

Yes, there are unlisted companies. And yes, not so many Japanese businesspeople use LinkedIn yet. However, there are plenty of companies that are listed, and there are plenty of Japanese people on Facebook, Twitter, etc.; so we should make the effort to do our homework before we meet the client. In this age of instant access to everything, there really are no excuses.

One of the other tricky bits about Japan is the group dynamic of decision-making. We may not know beforehand precisely who will be in the room. Because of the desire to share information within their firm, gain buy-in early with related groups, and spread accountability, it is rare here to meet with a single person. You may make an appointment with Ms. Tanaka, but often there will be extra people who turn up—so we won't be able to research them prior to the meeting. However, after the meeting, we can try to find out something about them that might enable us to establish a relationship. If the research indicates a particular interest, we might send them an article on that subject. In our case, we hand over copies of Dale Carnegie's books. If there are extra people in the meeting, we arrange for them to receive copies as well.

Gift giving is a bit of a tricky subject these days. I am somewhat conservative regarding individual gift giving in Japan. There are often internal corporate compliance restraints on entertainment and gift giving that we should be aware of. We don't want our efforts to cause the client any embarrassment or trouble.

Turning up with a prodigious swag of gifts for everyone would be embarrassing for the client as it implies you are trying to buy their business. Japan has a reciprocal obligation aspect to the culture and people are very finely attuned to keeping it in balance. Companies keep very detailed and accurate records of gifts they have received, the value of the gift, when it was received, etc., so that they can reciprocate at the right level. The object of this record keeping is to give something in return, thereby wiping out any obligation to the gift giver. If you suddenly enter their world and hand over a large number of goodies, it upsets the apple cart immediately. They must find a way to correct any imbalance, and an easy way is not to do any business with you!

On the other hand, we could bring something to eat—to be shared with the whole team—and that would be acceptable. Japan, fortunately, has an amazing selection of these types of goodies for just such an occasion.

As the relationship deepens, if we know they like a certain sport or activity, we might arrange tickets for them as our guest. Going out for dinner and drinks is also a tried and true relationship builder. Although, as mentioned, the compliance rules around being entertained by suppliers have tightened considerably.

This is the age of readily available, free information. We need to differentiate ourselves from every other salesperson out there. A simple way to do that is to spend some time researching the company and the individuals. When we have these insights, we ask better-designed questions, uncover more key information more quickly, and provide great context for our conversation with the buyer.

ACTION STEPS

1. Go online and read the corporate annual report.
2. Use social media to find out about the person you are going to meet.
3. Use search tools like Yahoo and Google to see what can be known prior to the appointment.
4. If new people turn up to the meeting, do a search and see if there are ways you can connect with them.

In the next chapter, let's look at client question design.

11—Life or Death Sales Question Design

To be successful, you need solid sales systems. Salespeople who don't have a framework for their sales conversation will wind up on the back foot, forced to follow the buyer's purchasing framework. By the way, the latter rarely includes anything about buying from you!

If we know what we are doing, we have built good rapport, used our Credibility or Agenda Statement (which we covered in Chapter Four) to receive permission from the client to ask questions, and are now ready to go deeper with our sales conversation.

The quality of our questioning ability will determine how well we serve the customer, which in turn self-selects us to continue in this profession. For salespeople, this is a life-or-death skill—get it right and you stay, get it wrong and *sayonara* baby.

For many salespeople who are "free spirits" and "artists," who never design the sales conversation, this usually means a detailed but meandering presentation wandering aimlessly through the nitty-gritty of product detail or service features.

Blathering on about the 50 available shades of pink, offering expert, in-depth insights into the differences, might be intriguing. But if the buyer is looking for blue, the effort is completely wasted and pointless. Now, this sounds primitive and obvious, except that the vast majority of salespeople are geared up for festive feature data dump, not for buyer needs exploration.

When I was selling Australian furniture in Nagoya, I visited a leading furniture retailer at his vast store. It was filled with beautiful pieces from around the world, with the notable exception of Australia. I wanted to ask him insightful questions, but he waved that idea away and asked me to go into my presentation, my "pitch." I saw that as a red flag, but had no choice but to proceed as requested.

I went into my explanation about the uniqueness and hardiness of the Australia timbers, the special designs, the opposite seasonality, and numerous other weighty and worthy points. His first question absolutely floored me. He asked, "Do you make furniture in Australia?" I immediately realised my sales conversation had assumed too much. I wasn't able to ask him any questions, which was bad enough, but I also realised that my actual presentation needed to start with selling Australia first, the manufacturer second, and the actual products last. As I rediscovered, poor sales conversation design leads to poor results. It pained me not to make a sale that day, but I did learn a valuable lesson.

There are some sets of filters we must apply to the buyer, to help us understand whether we can actually help them and, if we can, what type of help we should provide.

CLIENT FILTER ONE
We need to learn four key things from the client:

1. What they want (Primary Interest)
2. What they must have: absolutes (Buying Criteria)
3. What they would like to have: desirables (Other Considerations), and most importantly
4. Why they want it (Dominant Buying Motive)

The way we learn these things is to ask intelligent, well-thought-out, pre-planned questions. Will the flow of the client conversation follow this neat and prim order? Of course not! The client will wander all over the place, taking the conversation across multiple tangents. So what? This is to be expected in a free-flowing sales interaction. The key for the salesperson is to bring the discussion back to the key points we need to know, and to get all this information in the course of the conversation.

The tricky part of this fundamental idea is the ability to listen proactively to the client's answers. This is where many salespeople lack discipline. As we highlighted earlier, salespeople hear something the client says and jump right in, without letting the buyer give all the details. As salespeople, we are often notorious conversation choppers, barging in before the speaker has finished. Another issue with salespeople is that they lose concentration on the key messages, because they are so fixated on what they are going to say next. They do this because they fear losing that thought or that point, so they block out the client's conversation in order to formulate their own response.

Hey, here is some good news: Salespeople are allowed to take notes! Just write down the thought bubble, so it doesn't get missed, and sit back, relax, and keep listening to the buyer—it is that hard.

This sounds a bit counterintuitive, but the Primary Interest of the buyer is not what we sell. On a simplistic level, what we supply is a tool, a conduit, an enabler to fix a problem. However, what the client really wants to buy is much more specific. The solution, not the tool, is what they buy. Salespeople, however, miss this distinction because they are focused on the features of the tool and wish to describe it in great detail. Another sales mantra for you:

> **Clients don't buy functionality,
> they buy the outcome of the functionality.**

As an example, say you are buying a hand drill. If you have ever done this, the salesperson invariably describes all the functionality and features: weight, speed, power, battery life, portability, colour range, stock availability, the guarantee, etc. All great and good, but in reality what we are buying is a hole of a certain size. This hole is the end result we want and the drill itself is just a means to an end.

So, in this case, a professional salesperson's first interaction would be to ask questions, not to describe features. The obvious question is: Why does the buyer want the hole? Is it going to be made in brick, concrete, wood, steel? Depending on the type of hole, the solution will be completely different. Salesperson blarney and waxing lyrical about their super-cool drill is irrelevant. We need to know why they want the hole. What is the hole for? Is it part of a long-term project? Is it a one-off? Will there be multiple opportunities for a variety of hole productions? Are they going to be the only user?

Some common Primary Interests amongst buyers include: increased revenues, lower costs, faster speed, improved efficiency, more effective employees, and increased market share. These are all outcomes—benefits not features. The salesperson's job is to uncover which of these types of benefits the buyer wants. At the same time, we keep in the back of our mind how our solution will deliver these benefits. We'll use this a bit later in the conversation, when we get to that part of the sales process.

Buying Criteria are fairly straightforward. These are the features—things like colour, size, weight, cost, payment terms, etc. The buyer wants to know about the quality, the specifications, the warranty, locations, delivery, support, etc. If these criteria are not present, then there is no relevant solution to attract the buyer's attention. The client mentally dumps you and effortlessly glides away.

Other Considerations may not be hard-edged requirements, but they do influence the buying decision. This might mean special features, added value, special packaging, delivery options, delayed payment terms, creative solutions, etc.

As an example, selling up against one of the giant *sogoshosha* (Japanese trading companies) is a tough gig. You might have your bright shiny object, all ready to go for the Japanese market, but the Big Guys have a secret weapon. They have locked your buyers into payment terms that you can't compete with.

They may be giving 120 days to pay, so the buyer can receive and sell the goods before they even have to pay for them. You are looking for cash on delivery and wonder why you can't make any headway with this buyer—especially when you have what you think is a strong price advantage in the marketplace. What this means is that you need to know the full cost to the buyer, beyond just the initial price and where you fit into the picture. The only way to find that out is to ask well-planned questions.

In Japan, merged companies or joint ventures are often staffed with representatives from more than one company. Your contact may have come from one side of the merged business, but there may be other actors who come from elsewhere. They may have vested interests in using their preferred suppliers and not you. They may be driven more by existing relationships than by commercial logic or incentives.

When mobile phones first shrank to a size and cost that was less intimidating for the average user, I was selling steel towers from Australia to a Japanese joint venture company that offered mobile phone services. Within the joint venture, there was opposition to using us—even though our pricing was one-third that of the local suppliers. The reason turned out to be that existing relationships would be compromised if they chose us as the supplier. Although I can never prove it, I believe there was also vendor money under the table for those advocating the other suppliers. We got the business eventually—the first case of foreign-made towers being supplied to Japan—but the sale was almost compromised by Other Considerations.

Other Considerations can kill if you are not aware of them, so think ahead and ask really good questions to unearth them.

The Dominant Buying Motive is a compelling emotional reason for the buyer to make the decision to purchase. This is a tough one to uncover in Japan. Normally, these motives would include things like recognition, rewards, promotion, self-preservation, and self-fulfillment.

Because of the team focus of Japanese buyers, they are reluctant to tell you what your wonderful solution will do for their personal career, after it fixes all the issues they are facing. Often the decision is team-based—basically consensus on steroids. It is often hard to identify the "decision-maker" in Japan, because of the broad involvement of a range of diverse actors in the process. When you try to identify with your contact—what is in it for them—they will mention vague things like "the team will be happy."

Japan's famous *ringi* system requires that a large number of people approve a decision by affixing their seal to a circulating document. This typifies the consensus approach, whereas in Western models we can much more easily identify the key influencers on the final decision.

In the Japanese case, we need to get some sense from our buyer of who is likely to support the buying decision and who is going to oppose it. Our contact becomes our champion inside the company, and we have to provide them with the bullets to fire.

We can't expect them to do it all by themselves. We must support them as much as possible. They may be the buyer, but often they are not great salespeople who can carry a message well. Feeding them the talking points, particularly the benefits and applications of the benefits, becomes critical.

Subtlety in question design, sensitivity in the question framing, and observation of body language all become more important in Japan because, culturally, things are not expressed so directly in words.

In the end, you will never really know their personal Dominant Buying Motive. However, keep in mind what they have said and feed those same words back to them when presenting the solution.

They may have mentioned that hitting the targets would make everyone happy. Therefore, in this case, we might say:

"The training, once delivered, will provide the sales team with a greater ability to not only get more appointments but to get much stronger commitments to buy. This increase in revenue results will not only boost the level of pride in the team, but everyone will be also be much happier in their work, because they are succeeding."

It is not as potent as identifying the individual's personal driver ("because of the increase in sales results you will get that promotion you mentioned"), but it is often the best you can get. The key point is to align your solution's outcome with the points that they mentioned were important to them—be it as an individual or as a team.

Having built rapport, leveraged our Credibility Statement or Agenda Statement to receive permission to ask questions, and having pre-designed our questions with the buyer's four key interests

(Primary, Buying, Other, Dominant) in mind, we are almost ready to apply the questioning technique.

CLIENT FILTER TWO

Prior to reaching the questioning stage, though, we still have more filters to apply. We need to consider where the buyer sits. Where you sit in the hierarchy of a business impacts your perspective and influences your buying point of view. Here are some examples:

- **User Buyer:** They are thinking how reliable or easy this is to use.
- **Technical Buyer:** They are concerned that the spec be a perfect match for the requirements.
- **Financial Buyer:** The typical CFO, they are worried about the cost relative to the budget.
- **Executive Buyer:** The CEO, they are looking at how this solution boosts achievement of strategic objectives.

Being an astute salesperson, we will need to ask pertinent questions based on the specific interest perspective of the buyer.

The CFO, for example, is often less worried about the business hitting the top line of revenue than blowing out the budget allocation for spending. When we talk to the CFO, we had better be digging out the imperatives facing them. For example, when the CFO is only focused on the initial price, an explanation of the difference between price and cost will be needed. We do this when we get to the point in the conversation where we present our solution.

What is the difference between price and cost? Price is what you pay at the start, but cost is the lifetime impost of that product or service. If you have to replace something often, the initial price may be cheap, but once all the other costs (e.g. replacement expenditure, downtime during repair or maintenance, disruption to other parts of the business, management time and focus) are factored in, the real price may be much higher.

You may have paid more for something up front, but it lasts for a very long time and the amortisation of that initial price over many years means the actual cost is very reasonable. Breaking large numbers down to the smallest possible units should always be the goal. Salespeople should always be masters of the mathematics of time amortisation of costs.

The CEO is faced with meeting the long-term goals of the company. This means building the scale and quality of the business to reach those targets. The interests of the CEO are more often going to be focused on how to push through the changes needed to grow the business. We must find out what the strategic vision is first, then align our solution with the delivery of that vision.

The Technical Buyer is going to be very, very interested in the details. They are deep in the spec and mechanics of how the solution will work. Being able to nominate how the solution meets the spec requirement is fundamental to succeeding with this style of buyer.

The User Buyer wants to know how easy this will be to use, integrate, install, etc. They have specific needs and fears. In the questioning stage, we need to really do a good job of digging these out before we even think about talking solutions.

CLIENT FILTER THREE

There is yet another important layer, which sits across the "perspective filter." Often, we think that cultural norms are an important consideration when approaching the buyer. Americans are like this, the French or Aussies are like that; and in the case of the Japanese, you need to do this and that.

Yes, there are many cultural preferences that are important. The only problem with this type of cultural prism is that, on its own, it is often irrelevant from a sales viewpoint. Why? Because there are vast differences within a single culture, so segmentation is rather tricky.

They might all be Americans, but a typical New Yorker is not the same as someone from San Francisco or Atlanta or Houston.

We need to go a bit deeper and consider something more individual for our filter.

A good place to start is with personality styles. Numerous tools, such as the Myers-Briggs Type Indicator and DiSC, help us to analyse personality style preferences. Whichever tool you choose, it needs to be simple to apply in a sales conversation situation. I don't know about you, but I am not great at holding multiple data points in suspension, in my head, so that I can realise an "on-the-fly" analytical breakthrough. In the case of the 16 quadrants of the Myers-Briggs test, it means I have to mentally juggle 16 data points at once. That is beyond my capability.

I try to keep it simple. I rely on two decisions:

- **Decision One:** On a horizontal scale of low to high, where is this person in assertion terms?
- **Decision Two:** On a vertical scale, is this person more people- or task-oriented?

With these two snapshots, I have a simple construct and can try and place the person into one of four preferred styles.

How does this work? Pay careful attention to the person's speaking style, energy, tone of voice, and the strength of their opinions. Fast, strong, confident speech and body language usually indicates higher assertion levels. The opposite indicates lower assertion levels.

Also, listen carefully for the content of what they are saying. Do they talk about how the team will feel about something or do they focus on getting the results no matter what? If the former, listen for indications that they are more people-focused. If the latter, they may be more task-focused.

Actually, at different times and in different roles, we each exemplify all four styles; but we naturally gravitate to one more than the others. I am an Assertive/Task-oriented personality type. However, when I am leading, training, or selling, I move up the scale toward a more Assertive/People/Big Picture orientation.

When I am examining the P&L and balance sheets every month, I become more Super Detailed/Micro-oriented.

You might be thinking, *Isn't this leaping around between styles rather schizophrenic?* No, it isn't. You don't have to be carrying around multiple personalities, but you do need to develop multiple communication styles that are attuned to the specific personality style preferences of the buyers.

For example, the high-assertion/high-task style is the Driver. This is the typical "one-man *shacho*" (dictator company president) alpha personality type, who usually cares more about the outcome than the people achieving it.

Don't waste their time with small talk and cups of tea. Get straight down to it. Offer three alternatives, make a recommendation on one of them, get a decision, and then stop taking up their time (and get out of their office). Because they are so busy, they can handle direct, strong speech, and they appreciate getting back some of their time.

The polar opposite is the low-assertion/high-people style of the Amiable. They worry about getting everyone behind the direction they are taking, and carefully consider how the team feels about things. They like consensus and don't like risk. Cups of tea and "let's get to know each other" is a basic approach with them. By the way, speak slowly and softly, and don't sit or stand too close to them—we want them to feel safe, relaxed, and comfortable.

The low-assertion, high-task orientation is the technical person, the Analytical. They want detail, data, statistics, proof, testimonials, and validation. No fluffy big-picture macroanalysis for them. They want the hard facts, so you had better have your details ready to go. They don't care about how people feel, they care about the facts—just the facts. Speak quietly, confidently, and be prepared to field a lot of super-detailed (particularly what you may consider unnecessary, irritating, nitpicky) questions.

The polar opposite is the Expressive. They want to grab the whiteboard marker and draw out strategies, to create and brainstorm ideas off the cuff, to bounce concepts around the group.

Don't ask them for detail, because they are bored with "petty paperwork." They universally hate things like CRM or tracking systems, considering them a prime waste of time that could be spent more fruitfully speaking with clients.

More so than national stereotypes, understanding in which quadrant the buyer falls will go a long way to getting the sale, because you will be "speaking their language" and they will feel you are "just like them." You will be joining the conversation going on in their mind, using the language style they prefer. This is critical.

As mentioned earlier, you don't have to develop a schizoid personality to be successful in sales. All you need to do is switch your communication style for each group. You maintain your own personality, but recognise that selling the way you prefer only gets one in four people excited—and they are people like you. Selling the way the client prefers to buy, on the other hand, gets four out of four clients excited. The math's logic is unassailable!

CLIENT FILTER FOUR

With all this preparation in hand (and it takes about a nanosecond to complete this analysis, once you understand their role and their style), you are now ready to start asking the right questions, in the right manner. By the way, you will encounter similar buyer types and corporate roles every time, so it doesn't take that long to get a rough fix on who you may be dealing with.

A good place to start is to ask them where they see the business going. For example:

> *"What is your vision for where you would like to take the business?"*

This helps to scope out their preferred direction, the ideal outcome, the type of results they want. Once you know this, you need to be working on a solution for them that gets as close as possible to that mental picture. We call this the "Should Be Question."

Next, we ask them where they see the situation of the business right now, the "As Is Question." We could say, "How do you see the current state of the business?" Having established these two focal points, we need to start mentally designing questions that will show why having a large gap between these two points is fatal.

Why fatal? If the gap between them is insignificant, then why bother doing anything? Why take on the risk of change? If the gap is big, but there is no opportunity cost or no downside to not taking action—no imminent fatality to the business—then there will be no action and no sale. The client will just persevere with the current situation, do nothing, and ultimately not buy your services or product.

Whenever I meet with clients and realise they are not suffering in their business, I mentally prepare myself for the chance that this could go badly. There will not be a big enough existing gap between their pain point and my solution. There is nothing driving them to take action, so I need to work on expanding the gap between where they are and where they want to be. Often this is impossible, because they have little sense that they need to do anything different to what they are already doing. Happy buyers stick with what they have and do not venture forth to find improved solutions. In fact, we are the improved solution; but they don't care.

If this is the case, I don't try and beat them up and force the square peg into the round hole. I just thank them, leave, and go find someone who is hurting, who needs help to get their business firing on all cylinders.

Let's presume we have obtained the information we are seeking and have identified the gap between where they are now and where they want to be. We still can't proceed until we uncover what is holding them back from closing the gap between the As Is and the Should Be by themselves.

They know what they need to do, but why aren't they doing it? These are called Barrier Questions. They flesh out the issues and show how you might be the solution. This is super important because, so far, they haven't been able to solve the riddle facing them by themselves. A Barrier Question could be as simple as:

> *"You have explained where you want to be and where you are now. What has been stopping you from bridging the gap?"*

When the client tells us their problem, we should not assume this is everything. We have only met the client recently, so they may not want to reveal all their issues to a relative stranger. After they mention their issue, we should not just simply move on. We should ask a follow-up question such as:

> *"In addition to XYZ, are there any other issues holding you back or slowing you down?"*

Notice I gave them an alternative here, rather than asking for a simple "yes" or "no." If there is another issue facing them and they tell us, again don't be in a rush to try and close them. Instead say:

> *"I see, so apart from XYZ and ABC, are there any other challenges that are making it hard to move forward?"*

If we get a further factor, we now have to get a sense of where the real pain point is. So we ask:

> *"Of the three issues you have mentioned, which one would you say is the key and the highest priority?"*

Once we identify the iceberg and what is hidden beneath the waterline, we can start constructing a solution for that problem. Usually, if we can solve the major issue, the others will quietly melt away.

As mentioned, though, the actuality of having a problem and the desire to do something about it are not the same thing. We need to focus on fleshing out the Implications of doing nothing.

We must help the client realise that finding a solution is best done right now, without delay.

By the way, if there is no big advantage to taking action now, which means involving your brilliant solution, then there will be no sale. The classic reason for this problem is "busyness." They know they need to do something, but they are just flat out doing all this other stuff. They have no time to implement the solution they need. We have to highlight the long-term damage this short-term focus is causing.

I find this myself. People are trying to supply me with various goods and services, but as the president of my company, I am so busy that I don't have the time to focus on the decision I must make. So, I do nothing; and they receive no revenue, because there is no sale. Even when the leader delegates the decision to one of their team, there is little sense of urgency. In fact, the team member might resent being delegated a task they feel is not properly theirs. This is where we really have to work hard to draw out the harm of inaction. We must show that doing nothing is not a "no-cost" option, as they believe.

We must break through all the noise and carefully draw out the need for action—and action right now. If you are getting nowhere with this, then it is better to end the interview and find someone with a more burning problem in need of a solution.

I do, however, mark my calendar to re-contact them in six to nine months, because things change in business.

If I re-contact them in three months, not much will have changed since we met. If I wait more than 12 months, my rival will have swooped in and solved their newly emerged problems. Somewhere between six and nine months seems to avoid the worst of too early or too late.

We must remember that "no" does not always mean no. It just means that they are not interested in our offer today, in its current format, in the current business climate, at the current pricing. A "no" today can quickly become a "yes" a few months later, once business conditions change—be they internal or external.

Most salespeople are not sufficiently disciplined in keeping track of clients who have said no today, so that the connections can be nurtured. You need a well-developed system for tracking clients. Today, we can easily track and organise media that tells us of any major developments with a client's business.

This can be very helpful because it allows us to take note of any significant changes, which may signal that now is a good time to re-contact them, even if it falls outside the recommended six-to-nine-month timeframe. There may have been a change of management, a merger, or an acquisition. Any of these could completely eliminate the source of resistance to your offer. Sadly, they can also go against you, as your allies on the inside are sidelined or moved.

Returning to our lack of buyer interest problem, imagine the client has a problem retaining key staff. They are not all leaving at the same time, but gradually the organisation is seeing people whom they want to keep depart. To use our industry as an example, we might mention that we have a great training solution for improving engagement. We go through the tool in detail, but find the conversation doesn't translate into the application of our solution through a decision to purchase.

If this is the case, you have laid out the solution but there is no pick up by the buyer. So what can you do?

At this point, you might reference another client who had a similar issue and how the failure to address the engagement of key staff leaving led to that company losing market share and experiencing cash flow problems. This triggered a cataclysmic downward spiral, with all the staff now becoming worried about the stability of the company. All the key people began investigating escape options, eventually leading to the company closing.

Here we are fleshing out the costs of non-action to encourage the organisation to take steps to stop the haemorrhaging, and stop it right now before it is beyond repair.

Using the "feel, felt, found," formula is very useful when referencing other clients' similar situations. Having gotten nowhere

in our attempt to convince them to take action, I would apply the
formula like this:

> *"I understand how you FEEL about the current situation. Yes,
> some key staff are leaving, but not in big numbers yet; so, no
> immediate counteraction seems needed.*
> *"We had XYZ client, who had a similar issue, and they FELT the
> same way at the beginning because the departing staff numbers
> did not appear so severe.*
>
> *"What they FOUND, however, was that the missing productivity
> caused by the departure of key staff had a big impact. It took
> more time than expected to get replacements up to speed, and
> this situation was hurting their business. They saw a drop in
> revenue and a loss of market share.*
>
> *"This had a knock-on effect with the remaining staff, as key
> people became nervous about the viability of the company.
> They tried telling everyone all was okay, but completely failed
> to convince the highly productive, experienced staff, who could
> easily find another job. The departures actually accelerated.*
>
> *"Because the experienced people were the core of the business,
> eventually the company collapsed into bankruptcy and had
> to close. We don't want that scenario to play out, do we? To be
> safe, why don't we look at some training to build engagement
> and head off any trouble before it begins?"*

Having used questions to draw out the Implications of
non-action, we now need to ascertain the Payout for them. If we
deliver the solution and life becomes wonderful, what will it mean
for them personally? We need to be addressing the WIIFM—
"What's In It For Me"–construct.

As mentioned earlier, this is very difficult to isolate for most
Japanese clients, because they usually reference what is in it for

the team rather than for themselves personally. It doesn't really matter if, for cultural reasons, we can't get them to openly express the personal Dominant Buying Motive. As long as we get them thinking about the issue, that is enough. Later, we will reference these points when we present the solution.

We might ask:

"If we were able to stem the departures of key staff, how would the organisation see your leadership on this issue?"

If they are non-Japanese, they might mention their personal benefits: a promotion, a bonus, recognition, appreciation, improved status within the firm, etc.

If they are Japanese, they might say something about the group: "Well, the team would be happy that we remained stable and did not have to introduce a lot of new people they didn't know well."

At this point, we have gathered a lot of important insight and information about the buyer's situation.

Before we go on, here's one handy hint about how to take notes when going through the Questioning Model:

Divide your notes page into four sections and write one of the headers (As Is, Should Be, Barrier, Payout) on the top left corner of each box. As the client mentions a salient point, jot it down in the appropriate box. Keep going and just check your notes at the end before you finish to make sure all four boxes are filled with the necessary information. This way, you never have the problem of not getting all the information you require to proceed.

We now need to bridge into providing the tailored solution for them, and we do this with a Capability Statement.

Please note that we are not delivering the finite details of the solution at this point. We are just reassuring them that we have heard all they have to say, and we are letting them know we actually can help.

This is presuming we can help them. If we can't, we should say so and not waste anyone's time. Walking away from business because you can't properly serve the client gets noticed and noted. It says a lot about your *kokorogamae*, and people don't forget that. The time may come when they will have a need you can fill, and you will be the person they contact because they feel you have demonstrated that you can be trusted and are honest.

So, with the Capability Statement, we reference what they have told us and offer our solution capacity, addressed in terms of their Primary Interest and their Dominant Buying Motive.

The Capability Statement framework is:

1. Offer a specific recommendation
2. Reference their Primary Interest
3. Appeal to their Dominant Buying Motive

The actual Capability Statement conversation might go like this, using the engagement problem referred to above as an example:

> *"The engagement survey we have been using with great success here in Japan will help you to get a clear fix on the key issues that need immediate work. This will give us the framework for the training needed to address the retention issue. If we can do this, the key staff will stay and the firm's future will be assured. You mentioned the importance of motivating the team members by seeing no more departures."*

CAPABILITY STATEMENT ENDING: VARIATION ONE
If this were being explained to a decision-maker, who had openly stated their personal benefit in the solution (their Dominant Buying Motive), it would go like this:

"The engagement survey we have been using with great success here in Japan will help you to get a clear fix on the key issues that need immediate work. This will give us the framework for the training needed to address the retention issue. If we can do this, the key staff will stay and the firm's future will be assured. You mentioned the importance of motivating the team members by seeing no more departures. **You also mentioned this would make your bosses pretty happy, and a promotion might come your way at the next round of performance evaluations."**

CAPABILITY STATEMENT ENDING: VARIATION TWO
If they had spoken in more general terms about the Dominant Buying Motive, we might say:

"The engagement survey we have been using with great success here in Japan will help you to get a clear fix on the key issues that need immediate work. This will give us the framework for the training needed to address the retention issue. If we can do this, the key staff will stay and the firm's future will be assured. You mentioned the importance of motivating the team members by seeing no more departures. **You also mentioned that staff stabilisation would be appreciated by the team members, because they wouldn't have to deal with lots of new people they didn't know."**

In these examples, we say we have a specific solution—first the survey, then the training. This will stop the departures, thus addressing the Primary Interest. The Dominant Buying Motive will be either to get a promotion or make the remaining team members feel more motivated, depending on what the client has told us.

As mentioned earlier, if we can't actually help them, because it is not a good match, then don't try to "square the circle." Just accept that this client is not a buyer and go find someone who is.

Your time is too valuable to waste on people who can't use your solution. Schedule a re-contact in six to nine months, though, because buying conditions do change.

Having established there is indeed a match, we go into solution provisioning. It will depend on your product or service, but in Japan this is rarely done in the first meeting. We usually go away and come back with a written proposal or quotation that outlines in detail what happens next and how much it will cost.

The ability to set up the asking of questions, the designing of the questions with the specific audience in mind, and the ability to provide confidence that you have a viable solution is what sets up the solution provision platform.

ACTION STEPS
Client Filter One
    <u>Identify</u>
- Primary Interest
- Dominant Buying Motive
- Buying Criteria
- Other Considerations

Client Filter Two
    <u>Identify</u>
- Executive Buyer
- Financial Buyer
- Technical Buyer
- User Buyer

Client Filter Three
    <u>Identify</u>
- Expressive
- Driver
- Amiable
- Analytical

Client Filter Four

<u>Craft Question Design</u>

- Should Be
- As Is
- Barrier
- Payout

<u>Craft Capability Statement</u>

1. Offer a specific recommendation
2. Reference the Primary Interest
3. Appeal to their Dominant Buying Motive

In the next chapter, we introduce how to deliver the solution.

12—The Solution Design

We have made progress along the sales process continuum, building rapport and asking excellent, insightful questions. As we have moved along the questioning path, we have been mentally stashing away the solution building blocks. Now, we package up all this knowledge and align it with our solutions. We are looking for areas where there is a match between what the client needs and what we can supply.

As mentioned, if we can't deliver what the client needs, then we should be transparent and say "sorry, goodbye" rather than attempting to force a solution delivery, blowing things up in the process as we falter and fail. The collateral damage kills our reputation and personal brand. The short-term revenue in question is never going to be worth the gamble with your long-term reputation, and bad news travels faster and farther than we ever expect. Keep your *kokorogamae*—or true intention—clearly in front of you. You will never make a mistake in serving your customer, even if you can't serve them today.

While we were listening to the client, we were already silently sifting and sorting possible solutions to the problem. We are mentally scanning our huge floor-to-ceiling library of solutions to select the perfect one for the client. We now look for opportunities to tailor our presentation to the needs of the buyer and raise our value in their eyes.

Every rival salesperson will be claiming they have a unique tailored solution, so joining that crowd is not good enough. We need a differentiated approach that excites the client and makes them want to buy. The delivery of the solution must be bolstering our credibility, building value and countering possible concerns or objections—preferably always dealt with before they arise.

There is a simple checklist we must apply to our solution to assist in making the key points clear to the buyer:

✓ **Why is it important?** Having a solution and having a solution that delivers value is not the same thing. Where is the urgency within your sales conversation to convince the buyer that they should take action right now, to start receiving the value of your solution? We need to highlight the downside of not adopting the solution, in addition to explaining the upside.

✓ **What is it?** Is our solution explanation clear to the buyer, or are we overly complicating it? Always check for understanding. We often live in a bubble of complete familiarity with our own business. What is crystal clear to us may not be so clear to the buyer.

✓ **How does it work?** Is the rollout of the solution something that the buyer can easily understand, feel is doable, and interpret as providing value? Don't assume they will have expert knowledge on how you do things. You need to take them through the major steps and key milestones. If you can measure the ROI for your solution, then how this is done needs to be explained in depth.

✓ **Who says so besides you?** Salespeople are there to sell, and buyers always bring their scepticism A game to the sales meeting. We all love to buy, but none of us want to be sold to! Being able to refer to an authority—be it a satisfied client, a specialist, or a credible reference—helps the buyer open up to the solution.

✓ **Can you prove it**? Talk is cheap, especially salesperson talk, so where is the independent, objective data to back up these mighty claims you are making? Be very careful about making statements without the ability to prove them.

In fact, try to avoid statements and instead turn them into questions. For example, "We can deliver on time, every time." This is a statement the buyer may doubt, having been exposed to plenty of salesperson blarney, BS, and supplier hubris in the past. Instead, say: "We deliver on time, every time. Would you like to see our delivery logs, which show this consistency of service we have worked so hard to achieve?"

✓ **What are the most likely concerns?** Anticipate the questions the buyer might have so that you can weave the answers and clarifications into your solutions presentation. This will reduce the resistance and scepticism that may emerge at the end of the sales process. Try to head off doubt before it arises. How do we do that?

During the question stage, listen and watch very, very carefully for verbal cues or body language that indicate an area of possible concern that may preclude a "yes." You will miss these vital signs if you are totally absorbed in thinking about the clever thing you are going to say next, and are not really listening to the buyer.

All fine and good, but how do we actually pull all of this together? Let's look at six steps to set up buyer agreement.

SIX KEY STEPS FOR DELIVERING THE SOLUTION

Explaining why your proposal is the best for the client need not be difficult. We keep it simple and follow a proven formula. Here is an ascending six-step process that we must walk the client through to get them ready to buy.

1. Step One: Give the Key Fact or Feature

The first step is to raise a key fact about or feature of your solution. It must be specific, true, provable, and highly relevant. During the questioning phase, the buyer has noted where they want to be, and the facts about our solution must be selected to inspire confidence that we can deliver what the buyer actually wants and needs.

For example, if they ask about global delivery, we might say: *"We have offices in 100 countries."* The locations, addresses, and phone numbers of all 100 offices can be supplied, proving our claim.

Usually, salespeople are pretty good at explaining the features or relevant facts about their product or service. The vast majority of company-delivered, in-house training for people in sales roles is focused on product and technical knowledge—especially in Japan.

The Japanese buyer gobbles up data like a nuclear-powered vacuum cleaner. They seem to have an insatiable appetite for facts and figures. This is part of their mistake-reduction strategy. Basically, this is a common cultural trait, so you need to have a very good grip on the details.

2. Build the Bridge

Before linking the facts to the corresponding benefit, we need to set up a bridge to the new subject of the conversation. This is a very simple statement, such as: *"Let me tell you why our global delivery capacity is important."*

We do this because we want to separate the data detail from the benefit solution to let the benefit shine through. We need a bridge from one subject to the next, not only to keep their attention but also to make sure our communication is clear. If we have to get into a lot of detail in the first stage, then we need a breaker between that content and what comes next.

3. Introduce the Benefit

Having done this, we now introduce the benefit itself. This is a description of how any buyer can enjoy the solution that the fact or feature provides. We must clearly relate this benefit to the buyer's needs; otherwise it will garner a "so what" reaction. The benefit should also be substantial.

We are asking the buyer to make a change, to introduce us as the new supplier, to trust the unknown, unproven, and untested. Small scale solutions, no matter how good the benefit, will not be convincing enough to embolden the risk of change.

In the previous example, we introduced the fact that we have offices in 100 countries, built a bridge, then went on to explain why having 100 countries is a benefit to them.

VERIFIABLE FACT
We have offices in 100 countries.

BRIDGE
Let me tell you why our global delivery capacity is important.

BENEFIT
This means you can centrally design your solution and have it delivered at the same time throughout your network to ensure consistency across the whole organisation.

Sadly, untrained salespeople never get to this part of the conversation. This is because they are still babbling, getting out the sales materials describing all the possible features for the client to absorb. Clients need benefits as well as features to help them make a buying decision. Our job is to provide a clear summary of what they are.

4. Apply the Benefit
We now add value to the conversation by describing the application of the benefit. A benefit by itself can only provide mild curiosity value for a client. What they are really interested in is how that benefit is going to be used and how it will improve their situation. We all know that knowledge itself is interesting, but of little help unless the knowledge can be applied. When we get into explaining the application of the benefit, we enter the realm of the sales professional. The conversation would be broken up like this:

VERIFIABLE FACT
We have offices in 100 countries.

BRIDGE
Let me tell you why our global delivery capacity is important.

BENEFIT
This means you can centrally design your solution and have it delivered at the same time throughout your network, to ensure consistency across the whole organisation.

APPLICATION
The efficiency gained through this facility is immediate and substantial, because now everyone around the world is firmly on the same page. Common understanding builds more clarity in communication, and this reduces mistakes and time lost to fixing errors.

We are now leading the buyer mentally into the usage of our solution, as they project toward an improved future for themselves. In this stage, we need to be painting graphic, vivid, dynamic word pictures of a future state in which the solution is in play.

Taking the Application explanation for the service further, it would look like this:

VERIFIABLE FACT
We have offices in 100 countries.

BRIDGE
Let me tell you why our global delivery capacity is important.

BENEFIT
This means you can centrally design your solution and have it delivered at the same time throughout your network to ensure consistency across the whole organisation.

APPLICATION

The efficiency gained through this facility is immediate and substantial, because now everyone around the world is firmly on the same page. Common understanding builds more clarity in communication, and this reduces mistakes and time lost to fixing errors.

EXPLAIN WHAT SUCCESS LOOKS LIKE

"In your own location, you will notice the difference. After the team has introduced the service into their daily work, your usual walk through the office is transformed. The dark frowns of frustration have disappeared. The smiles on the faces of the team, because of the time freedom that has been introduced, will be creating a new company atmosphere internally. You can feel it— there is a real buzz amongst the team. They are more motivated, pumped up, and energised to introduce and execute what they have just received.

"You also notice there is more individual ownership. The phone gets answered faster and better, the energy in the meeting room is more dynamic, and even previously shy, silent staff are really confident to proffer their ideas. You can actually see that the commitment and engagement is so much higher than the week before.

"Yes, you are watching your differentiable competitive advantage in the marketplace balloon before your very eyes. People do make a difference. The pace of change is so fast, you feel it is like watching bamboo grow. The really cool thing is that this will be happening all around the world, in every location!"

Brilliant colours are powerful in art, and brilliant colours in word pictures are powerful in the sales process. We must present a brighter future through the application of the benefits of the details of the execution of our solution.

5. Supply Evidence

Next we must back up all this salesperson "hot air" with cold hard evidence. That does not mean it has to be delivered in a clinical, boring fashion. Some pizzazz is called for, to make our presentation memorable, impactful, and unique.

Evidence can come in many forms. It might be a **demonstration** of the solution using a physical prop or the actual solution itself. It might be an example, say a vignette, about a satisfied buyer whom they can call to verify your claims.

It might be the provision of hard factual **data**, something that backs up your salesperson claims. Test results, academic papers, and published articles by experts in respected media are all powerful evidence. It could be an **exhibit**, something the buyer can smell, touch, hear, see, or taste.

For complex explanations, an **analogy** is a useful means of making a point clearer. Using an analogy formula, we take something unfamiliar and link it to something the buyer knows well.

This comparison of our solution to the buyer's known and trusted world brings home the point very smoothly and is more easily accepted.

We might say something like:

"Hooking up the new FX3 server is like a rocket launch. It has full grid power acceleration on installation, moves to a solar power mode of sustainable low power requirement thereafter as it hits cruising speed and, with that in place, just keeps on going forever."

We have linked a rocket launch with a server, two unrelated objects brought together through this analogy to effectively drive home an idea or concept.

An analogy we often use for teaching our High Impact Presentations Course is to link public speaking to flying an aircraft.

"Giving a presentation is just like flying an aircraft. When you fly a plane, the start and finish—the takeoff and landing—are the most critical parts of the flight and carry the most risk. The same goes for speaking to an audience. Our opening must establish a great first impression, and we all know how critical that is. It must also break through all the mental clutter and grab the audience's attention. Our ending is about leaving a great last impression and is our final chance to drive home our message. We need to design that ending carefully for maximum effect."

Logically, flying a plane and public speaking are unrelated subjects, but we weld them together for impact in our message.

Testimonials are powerful, especially if it is in a video or text format, featuring known and credible authorities.

For example, on our website—japan.dalecarnegie.com—we have a 34-second television interview clip with Warren Buffett, the most successful investor of all time, raving about the Dale Carnegie Course and saying "it changed my life."

This is powerful proof—especially when it comes from a respected third party. You might not get Warren on the case, but you will have any number of satisfied clients who will talk about you, preferably on video.

We can put these on our website, send them out with our newsletters, and put them on YouTube, Facebook, LinkedIn, etc. Clients check us out before meeting us, and being able to reference strong testimonials helps establish credibility even before we meet them for the first time.

Statistics make great proof—when they are accurate, relevant, and timely. Sadly, Japanese government statistics suffer from a three-year time lag, which often weakens their applicability to the client's current situation. No one else amongst your competitors has anything better, by the way, but three years in business is a long time. You may need to look for more recent international figures that show a trend and extrapolate to where Japan is headed.

6. Test Commitment
Having walked the client through the solution process of fact-benefit-application-evidence, we are now in a position to test the buyer's appetite for our solution. It is also good to make sure that

what we have been saying is actually understood. We do this with a trial close.

Now, there are many views in sales on using the word "close." Authors like to debunk words like this so that they can differentiate their own book or model, which is fine by me. I am relaxed about the semantics attached to the word, because everyone in sales knows that the close is the commitment stage, where the buyer gets to make a great decision and buy what we are offering. So, I will use the word "close" here for the sake of simplicity. Apologies to all the purists out there!

The closing sentence is a question that seeks the buyer's opinion on what we have said. Here is an important difference we don't want to miss: We are not asking for the order at this stage.

The question itself coalesces the buyer's understanding of what we have been saying, as they piece it all together and start processing the content in their sceptical mind.

We want to get the balance of the conversation off us and back on the buyer and what they need.

It could be something as simple as:

"How does that look to you?" (visual types)
"How does that sound so far?" (auditory types)
"Can you see yourself getting your hands around this solution?" (tactile types)
"Does that make logical sense so far?" (logical types)
"How do you feel about what I am saying?" (emotional types)

Please note the difference in the language usage, depending on how the client understands things: visual, auditory, tactile, logical, or emotional. Listen for hints on the client's preference when they are speaking. Professional salespeople pay very close attention to word choice and what they are hearing. They then mirror the client's preferred style, because this makes the buyer feel most comfortable and safe.

DON'T TALK PAST THE SALE

Salespeople, please hear me! We need to be more disciplined. Don't miss this key point: Make sure we are only supplying the buyer with enough information to make it easy for them to buy. We often love to talk and talk and talk. The big talkers amongst salespeople always miss this key idea. Too much information makes choice selection more difficult. They have tested this with physical products in supermarkets and found that 30 varieties of a product choice did not sell as well as just six. The reason is simple: Less is more!

Diversion away from the main topic also creates greater distance from the buying decision. Blabbing on and on can lead to extraneous topics that have never occurred to the client. These can either cause unnecessary concern or add further unwarranted complications. Both bog down the sales process. Don't distract your buyer at the crucial moment of selection. Learn to have the client speak 80% of the time and you 20%.

After you ask the trial close question, SHUT UP! Purse your lips together, so that no sound can emerge, and wait for the buyer to react to what you have just said. As I have noted earlier, Japanese people are very comfortable with silence, but a lot of Westerners are not—particularly my fellow Aussies. They feel that the gap in the conversation means we are not in tune with the buyer. So, they keep talking in an attempt to restore the personal connection.

Japanese buyers are not constructed that way and don't feel any compunction to fill the gaps in the conversation. So, relax. Ask your trial close question and just sit there patiently, without saying a word until they speak, no matter if it takes until hell freezes over.

SOLUTION DELIVERY

Delivering the solution sounds like a straightforward proposition, but there are four considerations we must be aware of:

1. What we can do.

This is being very clear about what we can and cannot do for the client. Are there restrictions around quality, delivery, timing, and service provision that they need to know about now, so that there is no unhappiness later. Our goal is not to make a sale, it is to build a partnership with the buyer and make repeat sales.

2. How we say it.

The tone of our voice, eye contact, energy, facial expressions, and how we present ourselves come together to make a powerful communication cocktail. Uhms and ahs do not project confidence. Body language and our general manner should be confident, convinced, and reassuring.

If you can't maintain some degree of eye contact, and instead keep looking away and looking back again, in a Western context you may be seen as "sneaky" and untrustworthy.

But when talking to Japanese buyers, if you bore a hole in their head by staring at them continuously, they will find the pressure too intense and become uncomfortable.

Eye contact in Japan can be a bit tricky, because there is a cultural tendency not to make eye contact. From a young age, people are taught to look at the forehead, throat, or chin rather than the eyes.

We can and should make eye contact, but we may use it a bit more sparingly than in the typical Western business context. A maximum of six seconds is enough at one time or else it begins to feel intrusive. When you want to make a strong point, definitely use that six seconds of eye contact.

3. What we say.

Is it logical, consistent, credible, relevant, patently true, and congruent with how we are saying it? Like a best-selling author who trims the character's monologue down to the bare essentials, we should be doing the same with our conversation with the client. Trim our part down and amplify their part.

We are looking for clarity of understanding. When speaking in English with Japanese buyers, edit out all the idioms, your dubious attempts at humour, your foreigner casualness, and your inappropriate informality. Japan is a much more formal country than most, so keep it simple—formal but friendly.

4. How we look.
Our dress, posture, and intensity all impact the buyer in one way or another. If you have scuffed, worn shoes and you tell them your company is great on getting small details correct, the buyer will doubt you. If you dress flamboyantly and they are a conservative Japanese company, they will doubt your credibility.

If you ever turn up in a suit and tie and find that they are all in polos and chinos, lose the tie and take off your jacket. If you speak with a very serious, almost angry-looking face, they may resist the desire to work with someone with such an unfriendly demeanour.

Our level of excitement about the solution should be natural, not "circus tent" forced and carnival barker, huckster-like fakery.

If we were doing our questioning skills component of the sales process correctly, we should have managed to deal with all the key concerns when delivering the solutions part of the conversation.

Just to make sure, we should be ready for any objections or resistance to what we have said. Sadly, we are not perfect, and sometimes we only uncover the tip of the client-concern ice-berg. Rapport has not been sufficiently established, trust is not there, and the buyer has not given any indication of the massive objections sitting just below the surface. If client concerns do arise, there are proven ways of successfully dealing with them.

ACTION STEPS
1. Prepare these answers for the buyer:
- What is it?
- How does it work?
- Why is it important?
- Who says so besides you?
- Can you prove it?
- What are the most likely concerns?

2. Prepare the explanations for the solution steps:
- Feature
- Benefit
- Application
- Evidence
- Trial Close

3. Get our communication clear:
- What we do
- How we say it
- What we say
- How we look

In the next chapter, we will cover how to handle hesitations and objections.

13—Anticipating Hesitation and Concern

Eliminating client concern is a key skill for salespeople. We should welcome these concerns, because it is a strong indicator that they are interested. Buyers who raise no concerns can be like dogs that don't bark, but just bite you without warning. Or, to use another metaphor, buyers without concerns may leave you hanging out to dry. They have answered your questions, heard your solution, have no objections, but still don't proceed. You have nowhere to go.

This can be a most frustrating part of the sales process. Fortunately, this "no objections" Bermuda Triangle phenomenon does not happen all that often; but it does happen, and is definitely a formula for more salesperson tears at bedtime!

Trust me, after going down this "no objections/no deal" path a few times, you will really welcome hearing client objections in the future. You will be saying to yourself, "Great, some interest and something to work with here!"

When considering client concerns, remember that all buyers are averse to risk—and that feeling grows in relationship to the size of the purchase. Techniques for "overcoming objections" can confuse or mask the real issues.

This is not a tricky technique-driven conversation, a "when they say this, I say that" type of verbal tennis match. Rather, this is an exploration of the client's mind and what is bothering them, what is preventing them from adopting our solution.

Do we all buy solely using logic?

Actually, we usually buy on emotion, and then we justify that decision with logic. This is the point in the Sales Cycle to introduce the logic part to justify the buying decision, to help the client move forward with the purchase.

Whenever we sit in front of the client, listening to their concerns, we should be envisioning that "objections iceberg." For shipping, the cap above the waterline is not the major problem with icebergs. It is the massive, unseen wall of ice below which damages the craft. The same is true for client concerns: It's the big issues they don't or won't share that truncate the sales process.

Before we even turn up to see a client, we should have spent time preparing, running through things from their perspective. We will have made many sales presentations before this meeting, and certain consistent patterns will have emerged; so we can anticipate what will happen and when it will happen.

1. What might the client concern look like? How can we ascertain that we are actually facing an issue?
2. At what point in the sales process do these concerns usually arise? How can we anticipate them and be ready to deal with them in a professional, calm, collected manner?
3. Why do concerns arise? What triggers this process?
4. How do most people react when they get pushback on something they want to happen? How do we choose to react if the client pushes back hard on our solution?
5. What are some common concerns we normally face in these conversations with the client?

There is an old joke about English speakers dealing with non-native speakers. When discovering they are not being understood, the remedy is to speak more loudly! Salespeople can be like this. They find resistance to their solution, so they become more strident, speak more quickly, push harder—all in an effort to will the client into buying. They become very passionate, very agitated, very forceful. I have done it myself. This is ridiculous!

The best practice is to not react quickly. That is the point: don't react; respond instead. The distance between our ears and our mouth is so short and we are so quick to respond. We mix up the order. We go ears, mouth, brain instead of ears, brain, mouth!

We would be much better off just waiting a bit to gather our thoughts. We can do this is in a very fluent way by putting a "cushion" between what the client said last and what we will say in response.

The cushion is a harmless, vanilla statement that does not engender any resistance. It might be something very simple in response to concerns over a limited budget. For example: *"Yes, budget allocation is an important part of all firms' strategies."* This type of comment won't inflame the situation and provides you with valuable thinking time.

You may be reading this and thinking, "That's a cinch!" Trust me, it requires practice. We teach this to salespeople all the time, yet they often fail in practice—despite appreciating the theory— because their habits are so entrenched.

For example, I was once teaching the cushion idea and the salesperson seemed to grasp this point. But when we began the role-play, the first thing out of their mouth when the client raised a concern was a statement directly contradicting what the client had just said, as if the client was a liar.

In the role-play, the client was a potential buyer of advertising space in a magazine and had raised the point that there were no other five-star hotels with ads in the publication. The salesperson immediately shot out, "Yes, there are!"

I could hardly believe it—especially given this was just after we had covered this cushion idea in the class. But it is easier said than done, so let's practice before trying it on the buyer.

Use a cushion so that you can think about what you should say, rather than saying something you will immediately regret. Our first response thought bubble to the client's concern is rarely our best. Instead, we drop in a little cushion and then mentally go to our second or third considered response. This then becomes the content we use, when we open our mouth to speak.

We will come back to the cushion in a moment, but first we need to consider other angles confronting us. Before we attempt to answer the client's concern, we must mentally pass the ruler quickly over what they have said to decide how we should deal with it.

Do clients become emotional? Are they all perfectly logical? Are they all wonderfully articulate? No, they are not; so we must consider whether what they are saying is relevant or just **totally**

hopeless and off topic. In this case, we just ignore the concern and do not try to prop it up with an answer. Let it sink under the weight of its own ridiculousness.

If it is **trivial**, we ignore it and keep searching for the real concern that is holding them back. We might ask, "In addition to that concern, are there any other concerns you might need to address before we go any further?"

If the concern is a **total misconception**, then we should clear that up straight away and give them the proof that this is not a valid issue.

The client may be giving us a concern that is not important, just to get rid of us. We should recognise this and not bother trying to answer it. Just keep digging for the real issue.

We may have a rapport/trust build failure on our hands here and our perfect answer, to an irrelevant concern, produces no progress for us.

The client's concern might indicate **prejudice** against us. This is usually a perception issue, so we need to dig in and find out what is driving that before we attempt an answer.

Rival salespeople may spread untruths about your business. They may suggest you are in financial trouble and won't be around much longer, so the client should buy from them instead of you. This must be quashed immediately, and doubt poured on the trustworthiness of a rival who would stoop so low.

It is also possible that the concern is **genuine**, in which case we need to address it thoroughly.

We should think about the timing of the answer. Is now the right time? Should we leave it until a later date? Maybe this is a concern that is not important to address at all, and we should just ignore it and never answer it.

If we were doing our questioning properly, we should have been able to address these issues when presenting the solution, so that it doesn't even come up at this point in the sales process.

If we find that the issue is immovable, we may need to quickly re-run parts of the sales process. We may not have been skilful enough to establish our credibility during the Rapport build stage.

We should be honest with the client and admit that their concern indicates we have not fully understood them. We may need to explain that one or two additional questions are needed to understand what the client actually needs, not what we thought they needed.

Emphasise that we will do this quickly. The last thing the client wants is a full re-run of the entire sales process! We might say something like this: *"The concern you mention is an understandable one, and it says to me—and I apologise for this—that I have not fully understood what you need. Would you mind if I asked one or two more questions, so that I can really understand what you do need and see if we have it for you or not?"*

Following this brief re-run component, we may have to better clarify our solution because, obviously, we have not sufficiently explained how it solves their problem. Having revisited this part of the sales process, we try again with a Trial Close to see whether they are accepting what we are saying.

HOW TO ANSWER WHEN WE HIT RESISTANCE

Remember the "cushion"? Here is where it is important. We have listened, without interruption, to what the client has said. We give ourselves some thinking time by inserting the cushion statement, and are now ready to go to a well-constructed answer. We have determined that the concern is a genuine one, which deserves and requires an answer right now.

Our first instinct may be to plough in with our answer. But before we do that, let's hold it in reserve for a moment longer. Jumping straight in is not something a professional salesperson would do.

We are always better served by politely questioning what the client has said, to fully understand their thinking and uncover what is driving the resistance. Being told they don't have sufficient budget, we could go into a thousand good reasons why that is not a problem; but we shouldn't.

Instead, we are better to inquire, *"Why is that budget issue a problem for you?"*

A client rejected our initial training offer because they said the cost was too high. Do you get that particular objection? I get it quite often here in Japan.

Further digging revealed it wasn't a cost issue, it was a payment timing issue. That item would have exhausted their remaining training budget for that quarter. So, it wasn't the amount that was causing a problem, it was the impact on that one quarter. Obviously, being able to split the payment across two quarters eliminated that issue and we got the business.

I could have jumped in with a sterling rendition of the tremendous value that Dale Carnegie brings to the equation. I could have gone chapter and verse on the fact that our trainers have to go through 250 hours of trainer boot camp to become certified, that we have been operating in Japan for over 50 years, that our five-year average satisfaction rate is 97.7%, and so on.

I could have thrown the kitchen sink at the objection and they would still have had a one-quarter payment problem blowing up their budgeting, and they would not have bought. So, question the objection every time, before you compose and deliver your answer. Remember, there is no point talking about pink if they are really concerned about blue. We have to know if it is blue or pink they want before we can deal with their hesitation or concern.

After some brief questioning for clarification, we are probably bursting with enthusiasm to finally answer the concern; but we still need a bit more discipline, professionalism, and patience. Before answering, we should always ask about other concerns. We are particularly interested in drawing out hidden concerns. Simply say, "In addition to this point, are there any other concerns you have?"

We do this ourselves, don't we? We mask the real reason for not buying, just to get rid of the salesperson. This typically happens when we are retail shopping. We see a nice scarf and it is rather expensive. When the clerk asks if we would like to try it on, we say that we are just browsing, or that the material is too rough, or any of a thousand excuses instead of mentioning the real reason: We can't afford it.

So, the first objection we hear from the buyer might not take us to the real problem. No matter how well we answer the lesser reason for not buying, we will not be able to make a sale. We need to keep digging.

A variation on this approach is to test the validity of the nominated concern: *"I understand. Can we proceed if we can meet this concern for you?"* If they say no, then obviously answering that concern does not advance the sale very much. We keep digging by asking, *"Is there anything else that concerns you, that we haven't discussed?"*

If we hear other concerns arising, we should take the opportunity to bury the initial concern by asking: *"It sounds like this latter issue is really the key point, and the earlier one is not as much of a concern for you as this one. Is that correct?"*

Sometimes multiple concerns are raised. In this case, we can ask the buyer to rank the items by priority. Don't spend any time on the lesser-ranked items. Focus on the key item and try to remove it as a concern. Often, this one item—once solved—will mean the lesser items just disappear and we don't have to worry about them.

We zero in on the real concern by asking, *"What I understand is that if we can address this critical concern, you would consider taking this discussion further. Is that correct?"*

Solve that concern and then check again to find out if they can now move forward?

When we hear a legitimate concern, we have to decide what we will do about it. Will we deny it? Admit it? Reverse it?

We deny it when we understand there is misinformation clouding the topic. If the client says they heard we are going bankrupt or that we have some instability in our company— and that is not true—then we need to strongly push back on that nefarious assertion. We need to offer proof that it is not a real concern.

We reverse it by turning the concern into a reason for buying. For example, if the client says, "We are having a downturn in revenues and can't afford to shoot video for marketing now," we answer:

"Improving your marketing with quality testimonial videos now, while you are in a downturn, is the only way to get out of the hole. The sooner you show your real value to the potential buyer, the sooner revenues will improve. Doing what you have always done, in the way you have always done it, will get you the results you have always gotten. Now is the time to break that cycle. That is why we need to invest in shooting the videos right now to get immediate results for you."

If the concern is genuine, then we should admit it straight away and not try to fudge it.

As a buyer, nothing is more annoying than dealing with salespeople who cannot admit they are wrong. Weasel words, wriggle room, smoke and mirrors—pick your metaphor of choice, none of them work.

We are building a relationship of trust, and trust is built on honesty; so be honest and be straight about the problem. Today's concern may fade, but the memory of your lack of trustworthiness won't. We peg people we can't trust, dropping them deep down into our memory banks and resolve to never use them again.

When we address the concern, we need to craft our explanation with a few factors in mind. Remember, where they sit determines what they want to hear. Are they a User, Executive, Financial, or Technical Buyer?

We must think about whether they are an Expressive, Driver, Analytical, or Amiable personality type. Depending on these frames of reference, our communication style will need to vary to suit their preference.

We also have to go back to the questioning component of the sales process and recall their Primary, Dominant, Criteria, and Other buying drivers.

We need to weave in the available evidence to back up what we say. We go back to the continuum of presenting a fact, bridging to a benefit, showing how this applies to their business, providing credible evidence, and asking whether the concern has been vanquished?

If we have satisfied their concerns, then we move forward to the conclusion of the sales process: asking for the order.

ACTION STEPS

1. Don't jump in and try to "deal" with the concern.
2. Use a cushion to buy thinking time.
3. Run the ruler over the concern. Is it:
   - trivial?
   - hopeless?
   - prejudiced?
   - genuine?

4. Do we need to answer it right now?
5. Should we:
   - deny it?
   - reverse it?
   - admit it?

6. Before we answer the concern, ask two questions:
   - Why is it a problem?
   - Are there any other problems?

In the next chapter, we will look at closing the sale.

14—Designing the Commitment to Buy

As we know, clients are highly sceptical of salespeople and are constantly evaluating what they are being told. Buyers will provide clues as to how they are judging what they are hearing, and we must be attuned to those signals. Getting agreement is not a manipulative process, decorated with tricks and tactics.

By the way, there are plenty of people teaching such dubious techniques. That is the mark of the "here today, gone tomorrow" salesperson. We have our sales philosophy to guide us, and we use our *kokorogamae*—or true intention—idea to make sure we are on track. We are building professional careers and relationships, and we are not leaving town!

We should be sensitive to changes in body language, facial expressions, and vocal inflections on the part of the buyer. These are very culturally specific, and the same action may signal something completely different from culture to culture. The point is to be aware and to understand what you are seeing.

Particularly, look for impatience. We may have gone over the allotted time and the client may be backed up with meetings and wants to move on. But we are blissfully unaware, bleating away, oblivious to their concerns. Remember, we love to talk!

Are they really listening to us? Do we have their full attention or are they silently tuning us out? Don't be afraid to terminate a conversation and reset it for a better day in the near future, when you will have their full concentration. Nobody complains about getting their time back when they are busy.

Japanese are said to be "poker-faced" and hard to read. That is true up to a point, but watch carefully for their reactions and you will pick up valuable clues. Sucking air through the back teeth is a bad sign. This is an indicator of a difficulty or a problem having been identified.

If they say it is "difficult," either directly in English or through an interpreter, this is also a bad sign. I have worked with some

Aussies who have visited Japan on business, and as soon as they hear the word "difficult" they mentally say to themselves "no worries" and start working on a solution.

This is the classic foreigner salesperson "can do" attitude on display. Translating the Japanese word *muzukashii* as "difficult" is only partially correct. In a business setting, it is better translated as "impossible." When foreigners hear that translation, they get a better sense of the wall confronting them.

If you hear *maemuki ni kento itashimasu* or "we will investigate your proposal in a forward-looking manner," drink your green tea, get out of there, and go find someone who can buy.

This staple of Japanese expression is how they get rid of people without unpleasantness. I heard this for the first time in the late 1980s, when I was based in Brisbane and travelling to Japan to sell investment property. I was excited. "Great, we are on track to make a sale here," I thought.

But, I was soon set straight about this phrase's real meaning. I hope that we all do such a good job finding out how we can help our clients that we never have to hear it ever again.

Also, as mentioned earlier, be careful with the word *hai*, which can mean "yes." In business, it is the "yes" of I hear you, not the "yes" of I agree with you. We do it ourselves on the phone. We repeat "right" or "yep" or "yes," as we are listening. What we are saying is, "I am following you." We don't mean "I agree with you."

"We all like to buy, but we don't like to be sold to" is a constant axiom we have noted and are always well to remember in this sales life. To get the client's agreement to our solution, we need to get them involved emotionally and logically.

We have asked great questions, presented the solution in a compelling manner, and have dealt completely with their concerns. When we come to the Value Summary point in our presentation, just before we ask for the order, we need to use word pictures that show our solution's value to create a sense of urgency and extinguish procrastination.

HOW TO BUILD A VALUE SUMMARY:

1. Reflect on what you have heard from the client about their Primary Interests and what you have discovered about their Dominant Buying Motive.

2. Remind the client that they currently lack the benefit of your solution, and get their agreement on this point.

3. Remind the client that your solution is the key to solving their problem.

4. Paint a word picture of the future, where the client is using your solution, enjoying it, and benefiting from it. Strongly link this to their Dominant Buying Motive and how they will feel when they achieve it.

It might sound like this:

"You mentioned your concern about key team member retention and how it was critical to get the team motivated again. The current efforts to deal with this issue are not providing satisfactory outcomes. You noted to me that this was big concern for you, didn't you?

"The engagement survey that sets up the training will turn the situation around as team members become more confident in front of their clients, begin to see the deals rolling in, watch their names go up in big bold letters on the sales leaderboard, and find that targets are being checked off each month as 'achieved.'

"The motivation is now back, and the energy in the room is palpable. As you see their positive faces and more determined attitude, you feel your own fears of more key people leaving disappearing rapidly. Life is looking good again!"

Using steps 1–4, design your own value summary for your product or service. We are now getting to the end of the Sales Cycle. We have outlined our suggested solution and have been watching the client intently to gauge their reaction to our proposal. We have dealt with any remaining issues and have just delivered the Value Summary. We are now well placed to ask for the order. There are variations for doing this and, as noted before, the personality style of the client will impact the way we ask for the order.

Mysteriously, many salespeople don't ask for the order. They are waiting for the client to do all the work and sign themselves up. Why is that? Their fear of rejection is so tightly tied to their self-image and feelings of self-worth that these salespeople would rather lose the sale than ask for the order and risk rejection.

They do a great job of building rapport, questioning, and presenting a valid and credible solution, but then halt right there. If the client begs them to have the solution, then a sale will take place. Otherwise, nothing happens. These types of salespeople can make a living in so-called "route sales," where the client is a regular buyer and all the salesperson has to do is turn up and find out how much the buyer wants this month or in this buying cycle. They are better suited as "farmers" than "hunters" in sales.

If the client doesn't feel a strong sense of urgency, then the sale will probably never happen for this salesperson. Some other better-trained salesperson will turn up in the interim, explain the implications of no action, and ask for the order.

It is not that hard, and we are not required to be pushy about it. Here are some best practices for asking for the business:

1. If the client is a **Driver or Expressive** personality type, then a **direct** question is fine. *"Shall we go ahead and get started?"* They will not be offended by a direct approach—in fact they will prefer it. They want to make a decision and move on.

2.   If that seems too direct for the client in front of you, they may be an **Amiable** personality type, in which case there are softer options. We might suggest an **alternative of choice**: *"Shall we start booking delivery for this month or is next month better for your schedule?"* The selection of either of those choices means a "yes" answer.

3.   We might select a **minor point**, the acceptance of which implies they are agreeable to proceed. This is usually a choice they will have to make after the decision to start. For example, *"Would you want the post-service delivery survey results in a graph format or just as text?"*

4.   A similarly soft question assumes we are in agreement and asks about future actions, the **next steps**, that need to be taken. *"When would you like me to schedule delivery?"*

5.   To help the buyer overcome procrastination, we may need to improve the incentive to make a decision today, explaining the **opportunity** available. We might say, *"You know that our prices are scheduled for an increase from September, so why don't we get this done today so I can secure the best investment for you right now?"*
     This is often seen in retail sales, when you are told that this is the last dress in that size or the last tie in that colour and design, inspiring you to act so as not to miss out. Make sure that this is actually the case. If you tell the client some tale to get them to buy and they uncover your subterfuge, your relationship is toast. Remember, our goal is to make a re-sale, not just a sale.

6.   For highly Analytical personality types, the **weighing method** is appealing. This is sometimes called the Ben Franklin close in the United States. We take a piece of paper, write the decision which needs to be made at the

top, and draw a line down the middle. On the left side of
the sheet, we list all the positives of going ahead. On the
other side, we list all the negatives.

We help them list all the positives, let them list their concerns, and let them compare.

This is something I would only ever use with highly detail-fo-
cused buyers, because it can seem a bit manipulative for other
personality styles.

No matter which variation you choose, after asking for the
order it is absolutely key that you purse your lips together and
not speak. As we discussed earlier, silence for many salespeople
is intolerable. They feel obliged to eliminate the gap by filling
the airwaves.

They feel that silence shows they have not built sufficient
rapport with the client. Nonsense! The client needs some time to
think—so give it to them. Yes, the tension builds when you have
asked for the decision and there is no response, but keep still—no
rapid movements, no talking, no adding extra points, and no blathering to reduce the tension.

By the way, if you are ever selling with colleagues present,
tell them before the meeting to keep quiet during this phase of the
selling process. Once, I was asking the commitment question and
the tension was building. My colleague, feeling the pressure, very
unhelpfully began to speak. The tension evaporated immediately,
like the air being let out of an almost bursting balloon. I was left
high and dry, with no decision.

Instead, let the tension build. You want it to build, because
you want the client to end their procrastination and make a great
decision for themselves and their company. You want them to take
action and use you. Never be shy about providing value for clients.
Remember, clients in Japan have absolutely no problem with
silence, so be patient and wait for their response.

To illustrate this point, when I was working at the Shinsei
Retail Bank, I was in charge of our branch sales network. I was

visiting a particular branch and had been told by HR that a young woman there was having a problem with her boss.

I asked her what the problem was, and then shut up. For the next hour, we both sat there in silence. She was tossing around in her mind whether she would share her problem with me. At the end of the hour, she said she wasn't prepared to share with me today and we both left it at that.

Did I ever imagine this silence would last an hour? No. But I committed myself to not speak and to let her come to her own conclusion about sharing her issue. The point of this story, extreme though it might be, is that Japanese people are comfortable with silence and we must be the same.

Remember, the Sales Process is client-focused and is all about solution push, not product push. We are driving forward from a *kokorogamae*—or true intention—position of what is in the best interests of the client. We are looking to build a long-term relationship based on trust. We know that what we have will help the client, and it is our job to best understand exactly how that will happen and then make it happen.

The poor old client is not to be left to drive the process—that is our job. To get the best outcome, we must be the guide on the journey, helping the client through the sales process. If we begin and end with what is best for the client, then we will have many happy clients and solid repeat business.

If, after all of this, you get a rejection and are told "No!", harden up and deal with it. Here are a few techniques to help you keep your confidence intact when you get knocked back by the buyer.

First, use the law of averages.

If you have kept track of your ratios—how many clients contacted, how many spoken to, how many appointments achieved, how many proposals issued, how many sales won, average deal size—then you know your numbers. This will tell you that, within a certain number of proposals issued, you will win a certain percentage of deals.

We need to think about these outcomes differently. For example, rather than thinking, "I issued ten proposals and one was successful and nine failed," we switch gears mentally and look at the equation in a different way.

We take the average deal size, say $1,000,000, and divide each client proposal into $100,000 units. So rather than an all-or-nothing view, we see each proposal as being worth $100,000 regardless of the outcome.

When you miss getting an agreement, you say to yourself, "Thank you for the $100,000" each time. You also get excited because, with each rejection of your proposals, you know you are getting closer to the one which will be agreed.

Normally, after three rejections in a row, most salespeople crumble and crawl into a hole to lick their wounds, unable to continue the fight. We don't want to see rejection as a loss, we want to see it as just one step closer to a "Yes." So, rather than seeing three failures, we say to ourselves: "Great! Only seven to go before I make a sale!" We keep going through this process until we get an agreement.

I love the quote from the famous British Prime Minister Winston Churchill. It must become our mantra for this sales life:

> **"Success consists of going from failure to failure without loss of enthusiasm."**

Another method for dealing with rejection is to see the client as missing out. In my own case, I always approach the sale as being based 100% on the best interests of the client. I know that what I am giving them is the absolute best that they can get, and that it will get the best results for them by far.

If they reject my offer, then I think they are an idiot! These are not just fluffy words to make me feel better; I really do think they are an idiot. This sounds strong and insulting, but I honestly believe what I offered was the best thing for them. If they reject it, they are the one at fault, not me.

In this way, I never fear rejection and never crumble. Don't worry, I definitely get irritated when they don't select me, but I don't allow that result to create doubt within myself. I do try and think what I could have done to be more persuasive, but I don't allow the rejection to kill my confidence.

Sales is a roller coaster of emotions with massive peaks and dark valleys, lurching from one to the other in rapid order. You will not win every sale, so get over it! You must find your own way of dealing with rejection or else sales will kill you.

Let's face reality: sales is tough. Tasting the bitter ashes of failure is unpleasant. Getting rejected is normal. Get used to it or get out of sales! Here's another mantra for you:

"There is no failure, only learning."

ACTION STEPS

1. Ask for the order using one of these methods:
    *   Direct
    *   Alternative of choice
    *   Minor point
    *   Next steps
    *   Opportunity
    *   Weighing method

2. After asking for the order, SHUT UP!
3. Build your psychological wall against rejection.

In the next chapter, we will look at how to do the follow-through once the sale is agreed.

15—Sales Follow-Through for Winners

The implication of this title is that, if you don't properly follow through on the sale, you are a loser. Well, it is true—you are a loser. Getting the sale is hard enough, but the real difficulty is getting the re-order. This is where we should all be very finely focused. Rather than approaching a potential client with a sale in mind, what if we set off with the idea of the re-order firmly entrenched in our brain? This simple switching of gears completely changes the conversation, the goals, and the execution of the follow-through.

But, in a busy life, what often happens is that we have more than one client on the go. As we are completing one sale, we have others coming to fruition. There are proposals to write, meetings to hold, materials and data to gather—all sorts of tasks required to make the sale. In the middle of this rush, a sale is registered and the concentration on the future sales suck up all the energy that should be available to do a proper follow-through.

We need to think carefully about our workload and ensure that, above all, we protect our reputation for reliability. If we are going through the Valley of Sales Death, where we have run out of prospects and the sales pipeline is empty, we may be rushing around like a maniac trying to reboot the sales process.

This means we are often overextending ourselves and don't get to the follow-through in a timely manner. It might mean not following through quickly enough with potential clients we met at networking events. We lose the momentum and now they don't respond to us. It might mean that we have sealed the sale and have mentally moved on to securing the next one, without properly nailing down the execution piece of the sale we have just completed.

One key thing we need to check with the clients—be they someone we just met at a networking event or actual clients who have just purchased from us—is their expectations on the follow-through.

Clients themselves are genius at this. You meet them, hit them up for a follow-on meeting, and they say:

Contact me:
- *after Golden Week (May)*
- *after* obon *(summer holidays in August)*
- *after Silver Week (September)*
- *after* bonenkai *(end-of-year party) season*
- *after* oshogatsu *(New Year's)*

Basically, they are trying to condition our expectations of getting a meeting with them. That is to say, they are resisting our efforts to see them by trying to slip out of our schedules.

We can take a leaf out of their book, too, and make sure we set up the proper expectations for follow-through. If we are going to be busy, then we should say:

"Is it okay if I get back to you in a week or so, on scheduling our follow-up meeting?"

In this way, we are not putting too much pressure on ourselves, if we think we cannot actually squeeze in this next meeting reasonably soon.

If we have had the meeting, gone through our offer, and have promised to send a proposal with pricing, then we need to once again consider what time frame will allow us to remain in control and project the best image of trustworthiness and reliability.

We should say:

"Thank you for the meeting today. Would you mind if I shoot the proposal out to you in two weeks' time?"

If we have just made the sale, then we should be looking at conditioning the follow-through by saying:

"Would it be alright if I sent you the necessary materials you have requested in about two weeks' time?"

I struggle with this myself. I get on a roll and pump up the client meetings, then the proposals must start rolling out—and this is highly time consuming. The days are filled with more and more meetings and the time available between them to do the follow-up gets squeezed. Deadlines start to get missed, or start to drift, and things begin to fall off the table and not get done at all. I must have a few harsh words with myself and tell myself to stop biting off more than I can chew.

Often, the client will stall on a decision: "We will study the materials and get back to you." They don't get back to you—and you don't get back to them—to find out why they haven't responded as promised. This is because you have moved on seamlessly to the next client meeting, then the subsequent round of either hollow promises or genuine undertakings, which are slow to materialise. Salespeople, don't expect the client to do all the work on the follow-through—that is our job.

The first step, as you end the meeting, is to condition the client's expectations of what will happen next and when it will happen. Give yourself time because you want to reinforce trust, credibility, and reliability. Remember that, to the client, the things you promised in the meeting are just hot air coming from a salesperson. The real test is when we get down to the follow-through. How do you want to be perceived when it's show time?

Having set the time frames in a reasonable way—so you don't blow yourself up—you now have to really ensure that you deliver what was promised, on time, or even slightly ahead of time. Not too early though, because it will seem you were just sandbagging on your turnaround times; and certainly do not deliver anything after the agreed deadline.

They have given you permission to delay, but they don't trust people who can't make their own generous deadlines. Your trust quota from the client will start to evaporate. Remember, our objective here is the re-order, not just a single sale. You might worry about all the potential business you have left on the table by taking this extra time to concentrate on the follow-through with this one client. The trade-off is that your reputation remains solid gold, and you are going to ensure that you will be around for a long time, not just a good time.

The terms of the deal will have certain specifications, and these must be met. If you unilaterally decide to alter them, and then announce the fact as a *fait accompli* to the client, expect trouble. Flexibility is not a widespread trait here in business in Japan, so expect a possible client meltdown.

There are so many human relations complexities in play here in Japan, because the people we are talking to have promised something specific to others. If we don't fulfil our side of the bargain, then our clients lose face with their buyers. This is the modern commercial equivalent of *seppuku* (ritual suicide) in Japan. The clients are more concerned about their long-term position in the market, based on established trust, than they are about saving a few pennies on the pound. They will never deal with you again, because the risk is too high against the potential reward. You don't want that reputation—it will always come back to bite you when you can least afford it. In today's social media world, bad news travels far and at the speed of light.

You may have seen entertainment programmes in which the performer has many large plates spinning on a thin, reedy looking stick. As they increase the number of plates, they get busier and busier rushing around to keep them all spinning, so none crash and get broken. This is the sales life of follow-through. If we overestimate our capacity and launch too many items for follow-through at the same time, like those spinning plates, we will falter and crash.

We need to have a brilliant technology for time control and time management. We need to be highly disciplined. We need to be excellent memo takers to ensure we write down what needs to happen next. Never try to commit the many things you must do to memory, unless you are operating at the genius level of detail recall. There is an ancient piece of wisdom on this: "The faintest ink is superior to the best memory."

Write it all down, in detail, so that it is clear, there is a retrievable record, and everything can be put into action. We need to be able to transfer that information to our schedules and link it back to the required sequences of follow-through. These all add up to our completion of the promise.

Often, we depend on others for some parts of the follow-through, and this is where we need to be excellent at delegation. The main reason we don't delegate at all, and blow ourselves up, is that we are scared to rely on others. Somewhere in the past, we were let down and we are haunted by that memory for our entire working lives. We cannot grow unless we get leverage. The chief source of leverage is other willing hands. The issue with delegation is that we don't do it properly and then conclude that the tool, rather than the tradesperson, is the problem.

When delegating, there are some fundamental steps which must take place for us to be successful. Firstly, we need to plan the delegation and select the best person for the task. This sounds infinitely reasonable, except we usually select the person who looks the least busy. Later we wonder why we have trouble on our hands.

The next step is to meet with that person to explain the task. This is where 99% of people get it wrong. They tend toward the "dump it" approach rather than the "sell it" approach. The "dump it" approach is where they just hand off the task and maybe explain a few of the details. Typically, they just say, "I need this done by next Monday." They leave out the WHY and the "what is in it for you" part of the conversation.

Having explained the background, the WHY, their self interest in the project, etc., we now work with the person on the timeline and delivery method. We want them to be doing the main part of this, so that they have ownership and control over how they deliver it. There will be milestones towards completion which need to be monitored. At the successful fruition of the delegation, we celebrate the achievement.

Follow-through is not a one-time effort, it is an every-time thing. In Japan, there is no margin for forgiveness of an error. We are focused on the re-order, so we begin the follow-through in the way we want to finish—highly regarded as someone true to their word, who can be trusted and who is totally reliable.

ACTION STEPS

1. Understand the risks of poor execution after the sale has been completed.
2. Control the client's expectations.
3. Realise if you have too much on your plate and slow down the pace.
4. Gather the best time control and time management methods you can find, and use them.
5. Write it all down someplace where you can later find the notes.
6. Use proper delegation methods that lead to success.

In the next chapter, we will look at how to become a successful negotiator.

16—Characteristics of Successful Negotiators

When we get to the commitment stage, the client may not go for what we are offering exactly as we have presented it. They may seek to negotiate the terms of the buying arrangement.

We can't control the issues which arise during a negotiation or the attitude of the buyer, but we can control our own skill level and approach. The more we understand and manage our own behaviour, the greater the influence we will have. To be successful, we need to behave in a way that influences the interaction by moving it along a collaborative continuum.

Here are 10 traits common to the most successful negotiators.

1. Good reputation with good intentions
People may forget the finer points of the negotiation, but they will remember how we treat them. Burning people, being too sharp, too cunning, creates a negative reputation for fair dealing. Of course, the aim in business is to win. However, let's not go too crazy here—one deal is only one deal. Winning the battle and losing the war is for short-term transactional types. We aim to be around for a long time, so our approach will reflect that intention.

2. Respectful, trusting, and trustworthy
Getting to a mutually satisfactory and beneficial outcome is the goal. Along the way, we treat the counterparty with respect and they feel it. This adds to our own commercial history as someone who can be trusted in business, and that is worth a lot more than the contents of one transaction.

3. Confident and positive
Having the right intentions, our *kokorogamae* gives us strength to find a solution that will be well regarded. We are constantly looking for a way through the difficulties, seeking to find a solution to the other party's issues.

4. Well-prepared

Knowing the facts, the background, the individuals, and the market situation are all elements we can and should prepare prior to having any discussions with the counterparty. Being able to quickly source key information, as negotiations get underway, is a tremendous booster to finding a successful outcome.

5. Composed

Calm and considered is a good philosophical position to adopt in negotiations. Emotional control is a prerequisite for success.

6. Effective communicator

This idea often suggests being a good talker when, as we have seen, being a good listener is often more important. Asking excellent questions, and listening for what is not being said, is an approach that will yield rewards. Tact and diplomacy are skills that go a long way toward improving understanding and creating agreement.

7. People skills

Helping people relax, finding common ground, getting on their wavelength, are all people skills. Being able to remove barriers and reduce inflammation points, through how we treat others, makes the negotiation discussion proceed in a smooth fashion. We like to do business with people who are like us, and that is where the person with people skills really shines. They are able to operate on a level that the counterparty likes and respects.

8. Open-minded

Flexibility is a source of strength in a fluid, shifting activity like negotiating. Rigidity can lock us in to a position that precludes a mutually beneficial agreement, usually because we have let our own ego get in the way.

9. Creative

We are sometimes captives to our limited knowledge and experiences, and so the world of possibilities seems small. Finding a tangential solution through a creative approach can produce surprising breakthroughs when negotiations seem to be heading toward a train wreck. Thinking about a problem from various angles helps us to see options that may have been hidden or unclear. A useful construct is the IWWCW formula—"in what way can we ..."

10. A risk taker
In finding agreement, there is always an element of risk. Caution, timidity, and fear drive us into corners from which it is can be difficult to emerge. Having the capacity to take a risk, because you have thought through how to minimise that risk, is a big advantage when it comes to finding creative solutions to end an impasse.

Business is not a one-time thing, so how we treat others—and especially the way we do business—marks us out in the community. Bad news always travelled far and fast, but, as we have already discussed, in today's social media-driven business world, we are talking another level of transparency.

Successful negotiators know this and never let their reputation become sullied for a small, tricky gain. They play the long game and seek to permanently increase their influence.

ACTION STEPS
1. Create a good reputation built on good intentions
2. Be respectful, trusting, and trustworthy
3. Be confident and positive
4. Be well prepared
5. Be composed
6. Become an effective communicator
7. Develop your people skills
8. Be more open-minded
9. Become creative
10. Be a risk taker

In the next chapter, we will explore the negotiation process.

17—The Negotiation Process

Salespeople must be credible negotiators. Clients will often want to haggle or push on the price. The salesperson's job is to defend the price by asserting and proving the value behind it. In Japan, it is sometimes the case that buyers will expect a discount even when one is not warranted. They will push for it to test us. As salespeople, we must be well prepared for this.

"Winning is not a sometime thing. You don't do things right once in a while . . . you do them right all of the time." This is a great quote from the famous American football coach Vince Lombardi, and we can apply this idea directly to negotiations. Any business undertaking does better when there is a structure, a process that can create consistent outcomes.

As negotiators, if we don't manage the process, we risk becoming passive, reactive spectators to events as they unfold. Purposeful behaviour is the key to influencing win-win outcomes. Don't expect the client to do all the work—that is our job. We must guide the way forward.

There are four stages of the negotiation we should prepare for:

1. Analysis
We need to identify possible alternatives to reach an agreement. There are many levers we can pull in negotiating an agreement, and finding added value through those levers requires a clear view of our goal.

We need to see the negotiation from the point of view of our counterparty. To do this, we need information and perspective before we even get to the negotiating table. What position are they likely to take, what interests do they have, what forces are impacting them now or will in the near future? Who are the decision makers?

Do we have information on the positions being taken by the various members of the client's buying team? Often, in Japan, not everyone is aligned and the negotiation is an internal power struggle. A lot of decisions are collective, but the negotiators are unable to reconcile the contradictions at play.

This is especially the case when dealing with joint ventures and post-merger organisations. Staff are sent in from the respective parent companies, and there is not a great deal of alignment established yet. Some negotiators are provocateurs, there to sabotage an agreement because they disagree with the direction being taken. We can get caught up in this power play.

So, we need to do our research and reframe the conversation to avoid confrontation. This means looking for words and deeds that speak to a win-win outcome.

2. Presentation

We should rehearse the other side's presentation as well as our own. By doing a dry run of their presentation, as we imagine it, we may find helpful insights and ideas.

We should frame our presentation around the interests and needs of the counterparty. Talking about what we want doesn't move us toward an agreement. Speaking their language and contemplating solutions to their issues puts us all on the same side of the negotiating table, leading to better outcomes much more quickly.

When we present, we should be looking for areas where we can provide added value through our suggested solutions. This makes it much easier for the other party to agree, because the takeout is better or larger than they had considered.

3. Bargaining

We must clearly fix our BATNA (Best Alternative To a Negotiated Agreement) at the start. This is our fallback—or even walkaway—position. It should be realistic and as close to the ideal outcome as we can manage. If we feel negotiating "tactics" are being used on us, we can just respond by suggesting an alternative solution rather than getting emotional and reacting. Whenever we feel we are "reacting," we must change our mind-set to "How should I respond?"

In our presentation, we have tried to make agreement to our proposal easy. We shouldn't make the other party work hard. By being flexible, we can smooth their path to acceptance.

Having said that, your BATNA is not flexible. You are saying, "We don't agree with your request for a discount, and we are prepared to walk away." Not much flexibility on display there.

However, if you have a certain position in the market, your pricing will reflect that approach. Clients who ask for a sizeable discount are trying to forcibly reposition you. Your BATNA is there to say, "No, we won't be repositioned by you or anyone else."

You can only have this degree of confidence when you have the quality to back it up. When you know that other clients are happy to pay for your level of quality at that price point, this must become your standard of reference. If it doesn't, then you will find your price moving all over the place and your brand value will slowly dissipate.

In Japan, once you discount, that is the new price point. It is very hard to work back up to where you started. If you must discount, then make it clear that this is a once-in-a-millennium, supremely rare, planets-aligning, never-to-be-repeated occurrence.

Depending on how you do your pricing, you may want to build in a discount buffer so that the other side can feel they got a win. Japanese buyers like to go back to their boss with their "win." If your pricing is a published fact, then there is not much alternative to taking a hit if you feel that you must discount to gain their business.

Point out that you are bending over backwards to show them the value through this first exposure to your company. Once they understand the value, then you fully expect the pricing to return to normal levels. Or, if they expect future discounts, then you need to state that you will only discount for volume, following on from this first successful test purchase.

Being strong when defending your pricing may upset the buyer, because you have bruised their ego, stopped them from showing their boss how clever they are, or denied them their *kamisama* (the client is God) will as the buyer. Ironically, by being strong on price, you are reassuring them of the quality you provide. Only people who are very confident in the goods or service they provide are prepared to pull out their BATNA of walking away. There is a sulky, grudging respect for you from the buyer, although they won't tell you that openly and may continue to complain. If you feel that you provide higher value than the price being charged, ignore the pushback and move forward.

4. Agreement

We should make certain to specify all points that are agreed. Things which need to be fixed should not be left floating around— this is the time to fix them. So that there are no disputes later, we need to get the details down in writing. Each side needs to be comfortable with the document and clear about what is covered and not covered.

There will be milestones for execution of the agreement, and these must be specified. There will be a schedule for fulfilment of the agreement, and this must be detailed in scope. The execution component is usually where problems arise, as more parties who are affected become aware of the ramifications of what was agreed and may resist the agreement being completed.

We do better when we have a framework to guide us, and this simple four-step process will assist us in preparing for the discussion with the counterparty. We don't need to complicate things, but we do need to have a structure to help break down the complications into bite-size pieces.

ACTION STEPS

1. Do your analysis
2. Prepare your presentation
3. Establish your BATNA
4. Make the obligations in the agreement crystal clear

In the next chapter, we will look at how to become a successful networker to build your client base.

18—Sales Networking that Works

L eads can reach us in many ways. Ad words yield inquiries through our website. Display ads generate phone calls. Facebook promoted posts get the message out to a targeted demographic. Organic SEO helps our website bubble to the surface and gets people to look at what we offer. Crafted campaigns, distributed through our email list, get traction and results.

This is the world of marketing. We spend a lot of time whining about the inept capabilities of the marketing department, but what about we salespeople? What can we do to get more clients? Where can we put our energy and efforts?

In this section, we will look at the classic prospecting activities of the salesperson in Japan.

COLD CALLING

Cold calling does work; it just doesn't work particularly well, and you need a pretty tough hide to sustain it day in, day out. Plan your cold calling by targeting a few prospective clients who will need what you have and make yourself known to them.

In Japan, if you don't know the individual's name, then you will have a hard time getting to the decision maker. You can send a general fax or letter, but it will invariably go straight into the bin, unread. You can send an email, but it will be immediately deleted.

Instead, try sending a book, a free report, or a bulky gift by post. It will definitely be handed over to the individual you want to reach. The lumpier the better, because it stimulates curiosity.

Companies usually have a general number you can call and, predictably, the lowest-ranked person in the company—the one with the least authority, the least initiative, and the most-timid attitude—is the one picking up the phone.

When I was based in Brisbane in the late 1980s and selling to corporates in Japan, I was trying to build a new network of buyer contacts and had selected a number of targets. I was planning a business trip to Japan in a few weeks, and all I wanted was an appointment with the key person. The problem was that I had no clue who the key person was, so I had to cold call the general number.

This was in the days before the Internet, but somehow I found their phone number and was calling from my Brisbane office to the company in Japan. I would explain to the person (usually a young "office lady," no doubt forced to wear a company uniform,) who I was and what I wanted.

I would always be asked to hold, then get passed to the most junior guy in that section, go through the whole palaver again, and be asked to hold once more. At this point, I would get passed to someone slightly more senior and, with a bit of luck, might get to the person I should meet.

I was doing this in Japanese, of course, but calling a company out of the blue was still very much a character-building exercise. Each call probably took 30 minutes from start to finish!

The real kicker was that, at that time, I was working for Jones Lang Wootton in Brisbane. When you put that name into *katakana*, it is a total nightmare to understand—especially if you are receiving an unexpected call from overseas, from a foreigner speaking less-than-perfect Japanese, with an Aussie accent. Looking back, I am not sure how I managed to make those appointments!

Even recently, I was reminded how frustrating it can be to get through protective barriers in Japan. Our Italian colleagues from Dale Carnegie in Milano had won a global contract with a big-name Italian fashion house, and we were to deliver the Japanese training component of the programme here in Tokyo.

I thought, as a courtesy, I should call the president and say hello. I didn't know the person and, because the incumbent had just changed, only the previous president's name came up when I searched the Internet.

I should have known better, but I called the company, explained to the young woman who answered who I was, why I was calling, and what I wanted. "We will call you back," she said. Naturally, no return call was forthcoming. So, being stubborn, I called again after a couple of days.

I got to four re-runs of this pantomime before I said to my-self, "I am very busy, so forget it!" and delegated the follow-up to one of my sales guys. Ironically, we are doing a lot of training for this client and I still haven't met the president!

So, cold calling can be done in Japan; but you had better be supremely patient, super focused, and ready to strap on your seat-belt for a rough ride!

DOOR TO DOOR SALES

Tobikomi eigyo, or suddenly turning up to do door-to-door sales, is still practiced in Japan. Quite regularly, we have some poor sales-person, usually very new, turn up at our office trying to introduce something to us. They get trapped with my staff and never get to see me. I don't recall ever buying anything from such a salesperson.

Just to place *tobikomi eigyo* in another perspective—and to give you some inspiration about cold calling—let me tell you about the 106-centimetre-tall salesman.

Imagine you were so short that the receptionist couldn't see you unless she stood up and peered well over the countertop. Or that the typical unmanned reception phone and organisational chart are at such a height and depth that you can't even use them. This presumes you can even get into the building in the first place.

Toshiya Kakiuchi was born with a crippling brittle-bone disease that confined him to a wheelchair. He applied for jobs and found the going tough. Then, one day, a firm that built websites accepted him as an employee. He expected to be seated at a desk, building websites in the safe bosom of the office; but his boss sent him to the sales department. "You have to get out there and cold call offices door-to-door, *tobikomi eigyo* style," he was told, "looking for companies who need a website."

Seated in his wheelchair, he was only 106 centimetres tall. He found that many buildings were difficult to access because of steep stairs. His sales comrades were seeing 50 or 60 companies a day, but he was only seeing five—if he was lucky. Yet, in a short space of time, he became the top salesperson in that company.

After hearing his talk at an Economist Corporate Network event in Tokyo, I asked him how he managed it. He said that, with the limited number of calls he could make in a day, he had to really make every post a winner. He found a way to turn his disadvantage into an advantage.

As I mentioned, we also have *tobikomi eigyo* people coming to our office every month to sell us one thing or another. Like everyone, we send the lowest person in the chain of command to shoo them away (nicely of course, because we are Dale Carnegie).

Do we remember any of them 30 seconds after they have moved on to the next company's reception area? No. Kakiuchi-san, though, is definitely memorable, distinct, differentiated.

You are not going to forget him turning up to your office. He told me that he had to just keep going back again and again. Eventually he would get to talk to a decision-maker who could buy—and they did buy. The secret for him was to keep going back and not to give up. He was applying Winton Churchill's advice on how to deal with adversity.

So, if you need to do some targeted cold calling, do it and don't give up. Find a way to be memorable. If Kakiuchi-san could manage it, what excuse do we have?

REFERRALS

Getting referrals is also a great way to meet clients and is infinitely better than cold calling. Getting the referrals, though, can be difficult—mainly because of the way most salespeople ask for them.

"Do you know anyone who would benefit from my widget?" This is probably one of the all-time worst sales questions in captivity. Salespeople ask a pathetic question, get nothing back, and then conclude that referrals are too hard to get.

Change your methodology of asking and you will get a totally improved result.

A much better question would refer to a group of people that the client can visualise in their mind's eye:

*"Since we started working together, your business has really
made a great improvement, hasn't it? Can you think of anyone
in your golf group who also wants to get higher revenues like
you have, through improving the efficiency of the business?"*

This approach is more likely to get a referral, because we have
honed the potential client pool down to a small group. Use this
method and ask about potential clients from within their extended
family, their work colleagues, their range of friends—groups they
can isolate and see the faces in their mind's eye.

NETWORKING

Networking is a much more friction-free way to meet clients than
these other methods.

So how big is your database of contacts? How many business cards have you collected and filed? How many people do you
know? Turns out these are all rather pointless questions!

The best two questions are:

How many people know you?
How many care?

In Japan, networking throws up images of attending events,
exchanging contact details, and handing over *meishi* (business
cards). This is basically a push model, where you push your details
out to others in the hope that it will lead to business.

But what is missing? The care factor.

Yes, they have your beautifully designed and carefully
crafted message-laden card. But do they care? What happened
during your initial interaction that would create or increase the
care factor?

As the president of my company, I cannot cold call anymore.
My staff can, but being cold called by the president of a company
is inconceivable to Japanese buyers. They would seriously doubt
the reliability of a company where the president had to cold call

potential clients. They would see this as the job of salespeople, not the president.

Still, I need to meet potential clients. So, attending events is a great way for me to meet other presidents and start a conversation. In fact, I am attending events every week here in Tokyo and, like many others, belong to various chambers of commerce and numerous study groups.

Sometimes, I look at my diary and wonder whether I should remove the title "president" from my business card and replace it with "professional event attendee."

I am always fascinated by watching the way people interact—or don't—at these events. If I am correct in my presumption that people are attending the events in the hope of learning something valuable from the proceedings, meeting someone who can add value to their business—or both—then the current methodologies being applied need some attention.

Incredibly, there are numerous unfriendly, brusque, unresponsive people attending these events who are just killing their brands—their personal brand and that of their organisation. Some radiate "I don't like people" like a bad case of sunburn.

I wonder why their firms allow them to wander around alone, given what a force of negativity they represent. In their mind, they are there for the content of the proceedings, and meeting others is a by-product of the process that they clearly detest. It simply never occurs to them that they are the brand!

We are social beings, however, and today we are interconnected to the greatest extent in human history.

The six degrees of separation theory is already well proven. The saying "No man is an island" wasn't created yesterday; the idea has been around for a very long time. Yet, some of the people representing their firms don't want to connect. Dismal interactions are doing damage to the brand. We come away thinking poorly of the person and the organisation's culture. We judge the entire operation (this could be thousands of people) by how this one person conducts himself or herself.

We are not going to think how we can help them, nor will we bring solutions to their problems. We will never dream of connecting them to others in our trusted network or ever give them any business.

Others are more open to the possibility of expanding business through expanding their circle of friends. I use the word "friends" on purpose, since we all prefer to do business with people we like. We will do business with people we don't like, but only if there isn't a choice. Fine.

Question: What makes you likeable?

There are two networking aspects to this: the sheer number of people we can meet and influence, who will like us; and the quality of that influence. Non-salespeople reading this might be thinking, "Well, I am not trying to influence people." Oh, but you are! It is a truism that we are all in sales, whether we realise it or not.

At a minimum, we are selling an image of ourselves—trustworthy, professional, competent, reliable, friendly, intelligent, experienced, and creative. Being likeable is an advantage in business that we neglect at our peril. Drawing business to our companies and ourselves requires that we influence others in a positive manner.

Another mantra:

> **66**
>
> *You don't know which one is the beautiful princess or handsome prince, so you need to kiss a lot of frogs.*
>
> **99**

This is an old sales idea that is still relevant. By having a bigger circle of influence, we can generate more opportunities—so frog-kissing volume helps.

However, what really puzzles me is when, on meeting people who are in sales sitting at my table at an event, I discover that they work together. They are usually in pairs, but—shock horror—I have

encountered one case of five! I was really floored when I realised
one of the five was their section boss!

I would normally think that the company's management
team definitely needs some of our training, but I happened to
recall their president telling me a few months earlier what a
sterling global internal training programme they already have.
Just to really top it off, they were all recruiters!

If you are salespeople from the same organisation, attending the same event, divide up the room and get cracking on
being likeable!

A good starting point is to get there early and check all the
name badges lined up by the organisers for the day's guests (presuming they don't give you a copy of the list when you arrive).

This helps you put names to faces you have already met and
may have forgotten. It also gives you an idea of who is in the room.
There may be someone there in particular with whom you would
like to spend time. The event organisers can sometimes tell you
which person it is you are looking for.

After perusing who is coming, man the main entrance.
Because you are early, you can meet people you don't know as they
come in. Don't spend much time with people you are comfortable
with, just because you know them, unless they are already a client
and you are adding to the warmth of the existing relationship.

At foreign chamber events here in Tokyo, I notice that,
when there is a large Japanese contingent (usually a joint event),
the Japanese get there early and immediately sit down together.
This makes networking with them very difficult. What this says
is, in Japan, get there super early, stand at the door, and meet the
Japanese as they arrive. Do this before they get a chance to isolate
themselves. Japanese people always prefer to turn up early rather
than being late, so anticipate it.

When I attend Japanese events, where the language is Japanese, I notice that Japanese business people have their own way
of networking. You introduce the person you already know to me,
and I do the same for you. I rarely see Japanese people walk up to

complete strangers and introduce themselves. They are very happy to just stand around next to each other in splendid isolation.

This is a problem if you don't know anyone there who can facilitate introductions. You can ask the organisers to help get you started by introducing a few of the big shots in the room. Then you can work your way out from there. Somehow, when you have been introduced to the key people, there tend to be a lot of others hanging around them. This gives you a chance to meet these people as well.

Having been given the papal nod by the big guy in the room, you now have pixie dust on you that allows you to meet other lesser mortals assembled there.

Or, you can be like me and use your foreigner status to your advantage and boldly bowl up to perfect strangers and introduce yourself. The reaction is often mild shock, either because I am a foreigner or that I am a stranger—or possibly both. As foreigners in Japan, we are excused from certain societal limitations about how to behave. The Japanese business people in the room don't apply the same rules to us that they would apply to their fellow countrymen.

When I go with my sales staff to these events, I act like a battering ram to break down the walls surrounding the Japanese businessmen so that my team can connect with them more easily. There are lots of advantages to being a foreigner in Japan, and this is one of them.

What about my own Japanese sales team? Well, I tell them to harden up and go and break into those circles of people who know each other and introduce themselves. They find it tough at first, but gradually become braver and are able to do it.

Working for a *gaishikei* (foreign firm) helps a bit, too, because this extends some latitude to them within the normal confines of Japanese business culture.

How about the quality part of the networking interaction that I referred to? Here, the fundamentals of communication and people skills come into play. My observation is that there is also a lot of work to be done in these areas.

Some salespeople are too shy to walk up to a complete stranger in a crowded place and start talking to them. Ironically, you want a reasonably big, but not too crowded, room. Huge soirées can actually be almost impossible from a "working the room" point of view. The sheer weight of numbers makes the environment noisy, unsociable, and hard to penetrate.

So, to get you going, just walk up to someone and say, "May I meet you?" Look them in the eye and offer your palm to shake their hand. At the same time, introduce yourself slowly and clearly: "Hi, my name is . . . Greg . . . Story." Then start looking around for their name badge and ask, "And your name is?"

The typical position of the name badge—the left pocket—is unreadable for the most part when shaking hands, so make sure you attach your own badge on the right-hand side so that it is easy for people to see who you are.

In Japan, we are blessed with the fact that everyone carries *meishi* (business cards), so we can instantly tell their name, position in the company, and the name of the company.

Best of all, you don't have to remember the details because they're written down for you! I always like to look at the Japanese side if I am given the card with the English side up, because often the Japanese is clearer and easier to understand.

For example, General Manager in English becomes *Bucho* (Division Head) in Japanese, and the two positions are entirely different in terms of responsibility in a Western context.

For our Dale Carnegie Japan business cards, we don't follow the usual practice of English on one side and Japanese on the other. We all carry two separate cards. On the back of the English card, we list the following information:

TRAINING THE TOP 4 BUSINESS SKILLS
- Leadership
- Communication
- Sales
- Presentations

Also included is one of the principles from Dale Carnegie's book *How to Win Friends and Influence People*: "Don't criticise, condemn, or complain."

By the way, on the back of the Japanese card we do the same thing, but include a lot more information about the training content we offer. We do this because Japanese people are often detail-oriented dataholics. They love information—and lots of it— whereas most foreigners seem to feel that "less is more."

These details are all talking points. Invariably, when I present the side of the card with my name, position, contact information, etc., I am asked, "What does your company do?" With a silky flourish, I just flip the card over and start going through what we do..

ELEVATOR PITCH

Having swapped cards and been asked what your company does, it's time for your elevator pitch. A good elevator pitch includes a problem that everyone experiences, or that can be recognised as a problem. You make the point that you solve this problem.

For example:

"Dale Carnegie is a corporate training company. You know how, when people come back from training, they don't actually apply what they have learnt, because they are stuck in their Comfort Zone? Well we fix that problem."

Let's break that down:

OVERVIEW: Dale Carnegie is a corporate training company.

PROBLEM: You know how, when people come back from training, they don't actually apply what they have learnt, because they are stuck in their Comfort Zone?

WHAT WE DO: Well, we fix that problem.

Another example:

"Dale Carnegie is a corporate training company. Engaged people are self-motivated. Self-motivated people are inspired. Are you inspiring your people? We teach leaders and organisations how to inspire their people."

Again, let's analyse the framework:

OVERVIEW: Dale Carnegie is a corporate training company.

PROBLEM: Engaged people are self-motivated. Self-motivated people are inspired. Are you inspiring your people?

WHAT WE DO: We teach leaders and organisations how to inspire their people.

This structure usually leads to them ask you just how you do that. Now, if they are a potential client, **do not** proceed to tell them at the event venue. Instead, suggest that you get together so you can explain how you do this. There are too many distractions and there is too much ambient noise at these types of venues to have a worthwhile discussion. They may meet a host of other people and completely forget they were speaking with you in the first place. Leave the business discussion for their office in the next few days or weeks.

After the usual exchange of business cards, the usual questions such as "What do you do?" and "How long have you been here?" seem to be about as good as it gets. There is nothing wrong with either of these questions, but we can go deeper.

Letting the other person talk is one of the key precepts taught by Dale Carnegie. It sounds too simple, but there is a lot of influence and power in using questions and following Dale Carnegie's Principle Number Four: Become genuinely interested in other people. Reflecting on the word "genuinely" should make instantly apparent why this idea is so powerful.

Another good one is Number Eight: Be a good listener. Encourage others to talk about themselves.

We could try some additional interesting questions:

Where is the best local holiday spot you have found?
Which is your favourite restaurant around here?
Are there any hot spring resorts you particularly like?
Which foreign countries do you like to visit?
Why is your English so good? Did you study overseas?

These questions will tell us a lot about each other—what we think and what we like—and are always useful in finding points of common interest, which are the building blocks of being likeable.

I also recommend seeking advice from others. While we rarely take our own brilliant advice, we are usually geniuses at handing it out—and we enjoy doing so.

Ask the people you meet what they believe their company does particularly well. Ask how they build a strong internal team culture, especially if there are cross-cultural challenges. Ask about their view on the state of play in their industry. Do they believe the current market surge is a dead cat bounce? I think you get the idea.

Engaging people in a likeable manner builds brands, businesses, and a powerful network of people who both know you and care.

After meeting them, you might send them a quick thank you email; but this is pretty weak and ineffectual.

If you can attach a white paper, a link to an interesting article, or a short video on something you think might be of value to them. These follow-up activities are more impactful.

From the start of the relationship, you are looking to build your personal brand, differentiate yourself, and add value. Thereafter, connect with them on LinkedIn so you can keep in touch—especially if they change companies. Remember, it is how many people who know you and who care that counts, not how many people you know.

ACTION STEPS

1. Ask for referrals intelligently.
2. Get there early.
3. Check who you want to meet.
4. Stand near the door.
5. Don't sit with your colleagues.
6. Work the room.
7. Pin your name badge on the right side.
8. Simply ask, "May I meet you?"
9. Carry two different cards.
10. Don't ask obvious questions.
11. Use Dale Carnegie's human relations principles.
12. Send a follow-up note that adds value.
13. Connect with them on LinkedIn.

In the next chapter, we look at how to build a great sales attitude.

19—Your Morning Attitude Determines Your Performance Altitude

Getting someone to buy your "whatever" is fraught with difficulty. Sales managers and teams must succeed or it's game over. The critical component in sales is not knowledge—it is attitude. We can teach you techniques, product knowledge, customer evaluation, gap analysis, etc., but it is all to no avail if the required attitude is not in place.

Intuitively, we all know the importance of having the right attitude. Let's do a simple test.

You get up in the morning and open the curtains to find that it is dark, gloomy, cold, and rainy. Does this impact your attitude for the day?

Now picture the same scene, but it is a beautiful day—clear, cool, bright, and sunny. Does this affect your attitude?

If you answered yes to either of these questions, then uncontrollable outside influences have seized hold of your future and, at random, will determine your progress in life. Add to this random climate burden the rejection factor. As a salesperson, when a buyer turns down our proposals, even that bright sunny day rapidly sinks into gloomy oblivion. There are days when clients don't answer your emails, never take your calls because they are permanently in meetings, and have the audacity to say you are too expensive. And, it's raining!

Attitude is a choice. Great. But how do you choose to go for a sales success attitude over the usual negative alternatives?

Try these little darlings to shake off random attitude selection as your *modus operandi*.

BELIEVE YOU CAN
Sounds simple and complex at the same time. How do you build self-belief? First, find some small part of your work that you do well and start to add to that through study and practice. Identify and build on your strength. This is the positive path forward. Don't get

bogged down with what was wrong—that is looking backwards. Uncover what you do well, and look at how to be better. Always use the good/better formula to analyse what you have been doing.

We are not 100% perfect, and we are not 100% imperfect. Each of us is a work in progress.

Build on what is working and study what more needs to be done. As mentioned earlier, if you don't believe in your company's products and services, get out of there right now and find something you can believe in.

Bolt from Negative People

When losers gather for a "whine" party, don't accept the invitation to spiral down. Others can have a powerful influence on us, so choose to be influenced by those who are upbeat, optimistic, and permanently positive. Your job is not to reform whiners (that is Dale Carnegie's job!), it is to isolate and ignore the damage they can do to you.

Seek Out the "Beautiful" People

Move in the success circle. Suck up their energy and contagious positive attitude. Join the organisations where they gather and the committees they sit on, whether business or charity. A positive attitude is contagious—get and stay infected ASAP.

Embrace "Changetuity": the Marriage of Change and Opportunity

Accept that change is normal. Everyone wants the opportunities that change brings, but, somehow, they also want everything to stay the same. Good luck on that one; it won't happen. Change is a permanent fixture of life, so study how to become more flexible, adaptive, and considered. Be ready for opportunities as they arise.

Work Yourself Hard

Get up a bit earlier (uh oh!), get out of the house, and think while you walk for 20 minutes.

Allocate 30 minutes a day to reading something in your field (apart from the newspaper) that builds knowledge and stimulation of thought on your profession. Eat a little less at lunchtime and spend the additional time feeding your mind or brainstorming solutions. Watch motivational speakers on video rather than watching the news on television.

For example, I like Gary Vaynerchuk and his "hustle" philosophy. He is a total maniac workaholic, but he challenges me to get off my backside and get going. Find someone who inspires you to do the same.

Finish work and go to the gym—especially when you don't feel like it. You know that you always feel so much better afterward. Hone your mental blade during non-sales time.

Create resilience

Mistakes happen. Failures happen. Learn from these outcomes, and don't forget to analyse from only two viewpoints: what you did that was good (keep doing that) and how you could make it even better next time. Leave the negative approach—"let me review and concentrate on all the things I did wrong"—for your competitors!

Rejection in sales is normal, usual, ordained, expected, unsurprising. Understand that it is about the business proposition, not about you. Learn to distinguish between the two. As mentioned, if it helps to think that the buyer is an idiot for missing the opportunity your service or product value provides, then think it and keep studying for the next time.

Perspire from persistence

Mentally tattoo this mantra on your brain:

Dr. Story's Iron Rule of Sales:
A buyer's "no" never means NO!

It just means:

- not now
- not yet
- not this offer
- not this budget cycle
- not this particular buyer

Earlier, we vowed to return in six to nine months. Situations change, people move, business realities evolve. Never give up—always try again. But to do so, to do the necessary follow-up, you must be well organised. If your organisational abilities are a shambles, then fix them!

Salute effort, not just final victory

Don't postpone celebrating success until the deal is struck, the money banked, and the sales champions announced. That is too late. We need to be finding and celebrating the tiniest advances and collecting them like trophies. Success is the accumulation of small wins; recognise them as they occur. This is how you build a magnificent success attitude—one success brick at a time.

Purloin the past

Steal from past success to build a positive success attitude for today. Bask in past glory for a moment to rekindle your self-belief and gird your loins for today's battle with yourself. Here is some useful self-talk:

"You did it before,
you can do it again—got it—right!
Now get on with it!"

Live in day-tight compartments

I was once working as a painter and docker at Walker's Shipyards in Maryborough, Australia. The name says the job—we would paint ships, dock and undock them, and launch them when new.

As a ship painter, I discovered that the very bottom of a ship is full of huge room-size ballast tanks that are totally airtight when sealed off. Be like that yourself and seal off the failures, hurts, pains, and humiliations of the past. Don't let your past impinge on your today. Look forward, but don't dwell on the future either. You haven't earned that right, because you must get through today first. Plan for the future today, but concentrate on what you can control right here and now.

Build your sales success attitude and set up the foundation for achievement in all aspects of your professional life. Start with the weather, and make sure that you, not random meteorological circumstances, determine your attitude.

ACTION STEPS
1. Ignore today's weather.
2. Build on what's working.
3. Avoid whiners.
4. Seek successful people.
5. Embrace "Changetuity."
6. Hone your blade.
7. Reflect on good/better.
8. Remember that "no" doesn't mean NO.
9. Add one success brick at a time.
10. Purloin the past.
11. Live for today, plan for tomorrow.

In the next chapter, we will look at the impact of our habits on our success in sales.

20—Sales Success Habits

We are all the product of our habits. What we regularly do defines our level of success in sales. Bad habits, good habits—they are all the same in terms of the production line of results, so the input point—not the process—becomes very important for those salespeople who want to succeed. How do we ensure that we are adding good habits and eliminating bad ones?

Part of the input process is selection of priorities. Going to the gym rather than the sports bar is a choice. Eating a donut rather than an apple is a choice. Discipline is a famed part of military life, and various slacker generations are recommended compulsory military service as a way to fly straight.

Where does this military discipline come from? Regular habits are a big part. Doing specific things at precisely the same time each day, without variation, instils habits. Doing things that must be done, regardless of how you feel about wanting to do them, instils discipline, which becomes habit. You don't have to join the military to develop good habits, but becoming more disciplined is a big help.

Our biggest successes come from our ability to work with clients. There are very few professions where you can do everything on your own and don't need the input, cooperation, or contribution of others. We pick up bad habits that damage our ability to garner that input, cooperation, and collaboration. Here are a few habits we can eliminate if we want a smoother path to success with clients.

1. Don't make it your habit to complain to or about others.
When someone complains about us to others—and we hear about it—what is the usual reaction? Generally it's not good. Animosities arise and can linger for many years, as a result of what is considered an unwarranted assault on our good name.

So, if you want to create a blood feud, then start publicly whining about your sales colleagues. If you have a beef with someone, and you heroically decide to confront them with their failings, then expect either:

a.   the silent assassin, who won't say much but will be seeking revenge at the first opportunity or;
b.   the combustible, who will explode right there and then, and counterattack ferociously.

Very few individuals will look deep inside their heart, saint-like, admit their errors, and bow to your superior judgment. You have just made an enemy for life.

If the chances of success in complaining are so low, then why do people persist in thinking they can right the world by drawing the attention of others to their failings? Habit and a major lack of self-awareness are culprits. Find a subtler way to draw attention to problems that allows that person to save face. Call out the error of their ways indirectly. The issue will be raised, but not received with animosity. Make this your habit rather than a surgical, nuclear first strike.

2. Help clients to want what you want, and make that style of communication your habit.

When we are direct and assertive, it comes across like giving orders; and few people like being told what to do. We all love to buy, but we don't like being sold to.

Be a more skilled communicator and look for ways to stimulate self-discovery on the part of the client that leads them to see the wisdom of our solution. As we have stressed, questions are our friends and statements our enemies. A statement will trigger resistance, whereas a well-crafted question will lead to self-enlightenment. Rather than firing off statements like missiles, make a habit of asking well-thought-out questions.

3. Be a good listener and you will become more persuasive.

It sounds counterintuitive, doesn't it? Listening rather than telling your way to success. Hollywood has glorified the riveting, moving oratory that rouses the masses and points them in the same direction. In the real world of sales, listening is a useful skill mastered only by a miniscule minority. When we shut up and allow the client to speak, we learn a lot more. We uncover their desires, thoughts, attitudes, hot buttons, beliefs, fears, interests, etc.

By knowing each other better, we can become closer through improved communication around points of agreement and shared interests. It is hard to disagree with someone you like. The reason you like them is because of those shared interests and ideas. The reason you know those things is because you weren't hogging the airwaves and doing all the talking.

Remember your *kokorogamae* or true intention. You need to be genuinely interested in them. You want to make your clients your friends and business partners. Being a predatory listener, hoping to scoop up enough material to cunningly manipulate the other person into doing your evil bidding, is not a habit that leads to success. Clients are not stupid. They can spot fake interest pretty quickly. Those who wield the sword of fake interest will cut themselves as buyers realise they cannot be trusted.

4. Craft the appreciation habit

Self-centred people are always on about themselves, what they did, and how great they are in sales. They can linger long on their superior qualities and accomplishments, but are rather parsimonious about recognising the achievements of others. These people wonder why no one wants to help them and they get so little cooperation.

Flattery of clients is not appreciation. It is a lie that is outed pretty quickly. The fake praise alarm goes off inside the client's heads almost immediately. They hear it, so it has zero impact. It simply alerts them to never trust you, the perpetrator. Honest and sincere appreciation is what resonates with clients.

We know it is genuine because of the way it is communicated to us. General statements such as "That's a great result!"

or "Fantastic outcome!" are in danger of setting off the mental alarm. When we select the action or behaviour that was "good," we must make it real. Concrete examples add truth to our words and resonate with the client. Tell them exactly what they did that was good and it will be real for them. Instead of saying, "That's a great result!" say, "Getting a 15% lift in retail sales, in this current business climate, is a great achievement." Appreciate people as a habit and add in the detail of what they did well to make it credible.

We are the sum of our habits, and that sum determines our success with clients. Habits can be learnt and cultivated at any stage in life. We will definitely have habits one way or another, so why not make a conscious choice to use these habits to be better with buyers for a smoother path and a happier sales life?

ACTION STEPS
1.   Don't complain to or about others.
2.   Help others to want what you want.
3.   Become persuasive by being a good listener.
4.   Give honest, sincere appreciation.

In the next chapter, we will look at one of the most difficult challenges we will face: selling services in Japan.

21—Selling Services in Japan

You can't touch, hear, smell, see, or taste it; but please buy it! This is often the dilemma with selling services. More than physical products, services bring with them issues you ignore at your peril.

Japan adds a few more challenges, just to make the process more "character building." The service sector constitutes over 70% of Japan's GDP, so it cannot be ignored. What local characteristics should you take into account when selling services?

The buyer we deal with is rarely a purchasing specialist. In medium-to-large Japanese firms, people are rotated throughout the company to produce generalists. Promotions are given based on age and career stage, so staff progress along an escalator system toward management. Purchasing specialists are rather rare in the service sector. Also, training in Japanese firms is usually the on-the-job type, so that the limitations of the past are preserved for each successive generation.

Your buyer counterpart usually has a university degree, but invariably majored in varsity club activities, worked *arubaito* (part-time jobs), and had a good time rather than studying. Combined with the prevailing on-the-job-training system, this does not produce individuals looking to be innovators or risk takers.

If you are a new supplier, your buyer counterpart definitely puts you in the high-risk category despite all the wonderful things you bring. If you have no track record in Japan, all your claims are considered doubtful. Remember, Japanese buyers prefer the devil they know to the angel they don't.

Dale Carnegie Training has been in Japan for over 50 years, but we still get asked whether we have localised the training. We have more than 100 years of experience teaching adult learners, but we still get buyers who want to see the training first, because they doubt it is suitable for Japanese people. If you have a global survey, it had better have a separate Japan component—otherwise it will be seen to have zero relevancy by the client.

Years of experience have taught the buyer that the best way to make sure there is no risk is to do nothing. Buying your snappy service is counter to this, so your ideas are not that attractive. A more favourable price point is no match for inertia, and the risk/reward calculation is always under close consideration. In Japan, attaining a situation of no risk is its own reward!

Unlike in other countries, buyers in Japan generally do not consider consulting a paid service. Most people expect advisory services to be complimentary. This can be a bit daunting if such services are part—or all—of your revenue stream. Consulting firms here run into this issue regularly, and they must adjust their thinking about their offerings.

Often, the most difficult competitor you face in Japan is customer apathy about using your services. The perceived need to introduce something new, or to change what they have been doing, is not strong enough to advance the conversation.

A second strong competitor might be an internal team already providing part of the service you are bringing to the table. The people on this team fear for their jobs, and thus do their best to keep you out—even though what you offer would improve the competitiveness of the operation.

I met an absolute master of this technique, a man who oversaw internal training for a prominent foreign pharmaceuticals company. I had met the foreign president of this company at a networking function, and was following up by meeting with his head of training. When I met the head of training, the president was in the room with him; but because the trainer's English was poor, we spoke Japanese. This meant his boss couldn't understand what we were talking about.

This intrepid head of internal training also had his team members with him in the meeting. He cleverly faked objectivity about my offer, and then damned me with faint praise. It was delivered in such a skilful manner that it was devastating and surreal at the same time.

I felt like I was witnessing a slow-motion train wreck;

and I was the driver. The performance was so perfect, I briefly considered giving him a sardonic standing ovation. Obviously, no sale that day—or any other, while he is still the puppet master at that company.

Existing suppliers represent a third potential competitor. In this case, trust has been built deep into the existing relationship; and Japanese firms generally prefer predictability to the unknown. It is hard to compete with an existing relationship—especially one that started with the buyer's grandfather being entertained by the supplier's grandfather more than 80 years ago! There are many multigenerational heads of business in Japan, so these relationship rivers run wide and deep.

With so many intangibles revolving around the service offering you provide, applying leverage and wedging your way in can be challenging.

Unhelpfully, in many companies the buyers are moved every few years as they rotate through various positions in their organisations. That buyer you have fervently educated about your service offering gets moved and replaced by someone who has their own networks or wants to do things differently. Neither of these latter options involves you, unfortunately, so you must kiss that business goodbye until the next rotation.

The reverse works in your favour sometimes, as Mr. or Ms. Rude and Unhelpful gets shunted off elsewhere and someone useful turns up. Sadly, in my experience, the moves are usually more painful than helpful.

Depending on the size of your operation, media in Japan may be useful for getting out the message about your services. Larger firms have better leverage opportunities than smaller operations when it comes to haggling over ad pricing.

Establishing brand awareness in Japan relies on sustainability. Spot activities may work, but usually "water on rock" continuity is what is required here; and that is expensive.

Public relations activities may be a better alternative. Japanese media is highly competitive, and journalists are super busy people, so your story might get a run. The downside cost of trying and failing is not very high, so it may be worth a shot.

Another good idea is improving your sales effort to overcome all these character-building challenges I have listed. Your competitor's sales team may be poorly skilled and poorly led. Very few salespeople are properly trained in Japan, and if on-the-job training has been their total curriculum, they will likely underperform. It is also a rare bird of a sales manager in Japan who is actually competent and can properly lead a team.

At Dale Carnegie, we do a lot of sales training across all industries—including services—and often the foreign company president struggles to understand why sales are not satisfactory. The answer is usually that the Japanese salespeople have relied on relationships and big-name branding to make the sale, rather than applying any sales acumen.

A skilled team of questioners will definitely outperform the competition, simply because the standard is generally so low. Even a half-baked sales process is better than none, and is usually what your rivals bring to the table: no process and lots of winging it.

You can't control the cost of media, the rotation of generalists, the buyer's risk aversion, or what your various competitors are doing, but you can control what you are doing. Take a cold, hard look at your sales results and really dig into how you are approaching the sale. Then get proper sales training. This may be the area where you can have the biggest, fastest impact.

ACTION STEPS
1. Don't forget: services are a big chunk of the economy.
2. Expect buyer apathy.
3. Have your objection handling fine-tuned—you'll need it.
4. Wait out hopeless purchasing officers.
5. Use media exposure to build credibility.
6. Get proper sales training.

In the next chapter, we will address that age-old enemy of success: salesperson procrastination.

22—Tips for Overcoming Procrastination

Salespeople hate paperwork. They are usually Expressive personality types who are assertive and love being with people. They are big-picture people, and doing the paperwork for things like CRM bores them to tears. But it must be done—especially in today's business world, where every client is carefully segmented so that the Marketing Team can appeal to them in the most effective way.

Inner dialogue on doing things we don't want to do could be an issue. We are talking ourselves out of doing the work because of what we are saying to ourselves about the prospect ahead: boredom. Here are some ideas for changing the inner conversation, to slip the chains of procrastination and help get the hard bits completed.

1. *"I need to do it perfectly."*
Our perfectionism is holding us back. Japanese society really emphasises doing things correctly, and there is a low tolerance for mistakes. We can say instead:

> *"I will get this project started and give myself sufficient time to work on it, so that it is done correctly."*

2. *"I have to."*
Our feelings of resistance increase whenever the words "have to" appear. We want to demonstrate our fierce independence by rejecting the "have to" imperative and showing that project who is boss. Sadly, we still don't start; so it's all a bit self-defeating in the end. Let's take back control and instead say:

> *"I choose to."*

3. *"This project is overwhelming."*
This is the "eat the elephant" (one bite at a time) or "eat the live frog" (swallow in one gulp) metaphor. We are put off by the size or

difficulty of the task at hand. Our mind is doing a quick calculation of all the other things we have to do. The idea of one project sucking up all our time is not computing. Let's change our focus from contemplating the project in its entirety and say to ourselves:

> *"Where is the best place to start."*

4. *"I don't even have time for lunch."*
Occasionally, this may happen; but if it is your regular excuse for not getting projects done, then we need to confront it head-on. Change the focus to yourself and say:

> *"My work effectiveness will be much, much better after a break, so I will take lunch and then really get into it."*

5. *"I'll never get this finished."*
The prospect of completion is so daunting that we run up the white flag immediately. We can see an ocean of pain spreading out before us, and we want to delay the onset. Rather, let's talk ourselves into it by noting:

> *"I know that once I get started, I will be on a roll."*

6. *"There is no way I can succeed."*
This is another one of those "all or nothing" choices we make. If I can't do it perfectly, better not to do it at all. We tell ourselves that it is better to avoid failure and not to confront our inner demons. So, we simply don't start. Switch gears and use a *kaizen* thought process:

> *"I will give it my best shot, get it going, and work on improving it along the way."*

7. *"No one else is working as hard as me."*
Our self-talk can become a problem. "Being such a legend in the

workplace, I deserve to be cut some slack around here," we tell ourselves. "I can cruise for a bit, because I am more valuable than the rest of the crew." Hello, self-indulgent super salesperson! Give me a break! Look at it differently:

"This is my chance to take a leadership role and encourage others to swallow their frog."

8. *"I don't know where to begin."*
A towering wall of rock is confronting us. Looking straight up, it is a long way to the top. Switch thoughts and say:

"Get the hard part done and then the rest will be easy."

9. *"I hate this part of the job."*
We know ourselves, and we know our pain and pleasure points. Let's combine them and think:

"Once I finish this task, I will reward myself!"

By changing our inner conversation, we change our productivity. Remember, time is limited. We can't do everything, but we can choose to do the most important thing every day. Let's talk ourselves into it.

ACTION STEPS
1. Change our thinking.
2. Change our self-talk.

In the next chapter, we will look at bad clients and what to do about them.

23—Buyers Behaving Badly

T he customer is *kamisama* (God) in sales in Japan. We hear this a lot across all industries and sectors. Sometimes, however, the buyer can more like an *oni* (demon) when they deal with salespeople. Bad behaviour is bad behaviour, regardless of the source; but when you are trying to sell a company on your product or service, do you just have to suck it up? Actually, no!

Unless you are in a very small market segment with a limited number of buyers, then, as a salesperson, you have choices. If the former is the case, I suggest changing industries and getting out of that negative, bad-behaviour environment. Life is short, and good salespeople have highly transferable skills. If you know what you are doing, you can work in almost any business—as long as there is no requirement for highly developed technical knowledge.

The Japan winner of the worst sales environment is the pharmaceutical industry, selling to doctors.

Unlike the rest of the advanced world, where patients use the Internet to educate themselves about medical conditions before they see the doctor, Japan is stuck in the pre-1990s. Consequently, Japanese doctors still consider themselves vastly superior to everyone else, from patients on down.

At the absolute bottom of the pile are drug salespeople, being forced to wait around for hours, fawning over the doctor, being spoken to like dirt, cleaning their Mercedes, arranging all types of incentives to get them to buy. This poor buyer behaviour towards pharma salespeople has been legendary for decades.

Recently, conflicts of interest have emerged, and there are now many more restrictions on entertaining doctors. The goodies are being restricted, and so the salesperson doesn't have much in the way of *ame* (sweets) to offer anymore. They still get plenty of *muchi* (whip) from the buyer though.

Japanese society has a powerful hierarchy. When the company president tells their staff to get together with you, the salesperson, you might be thinking, "this is looking good." Not necessarily.

What often surprises me about managers in Japan is how they run their own show, regardless of what the president may want.

I had lunch with the president of a multinational company who was running the Japan operation. This leader was dynamic, articulate, and a great presenter. After lunch, as promised, the president sent an email to the manager instructing them to get together with me to discuss training for their company. I followed up with the manager many times, but never got an answer. It became obvious that they did not care what the president said. They had their own views on how to run their show—and I did not fit into that plan.

Telling the president who introduced you that, in fact, they have no power within their own organisation is a bit of a delicate conversation. If you raise it, you have just said that the emperor has no clothes. They do not thank you for pointing out that their manager is rebellious and they themselves are impotent.

Another annoying activity is being asked to spend time preparing a quote when there is no intention to buy from you. This is often driven by the compliance division with internal rules requiring three quotes. They have already secretly selected the provider, and your job is to provide the paperwork to make sure that happens.

We were contacted by a large company asking for a quote on a particular aspect of training. Efforts to meet the client to discuss their needs were rebuffed; they said they were so busy. "Just send the quote, it will be fine," we were told. This is a tricky one, because you don't know if you are the patsy or if they are, in fact, so very busy and that is why they need your help.

In these cases, to test the system, I never follow up from my side after sending the quote. Sounds like a bad sales effort—and maybe I should be fired—but it is a technique to reveal if we are dealing with a time waster or a genuine buyer.

If they are really interested, they will respond with either more questions or an order. If stony silence is all we get, then we know that we have been royally used to assist a competitor's sales effort. That is a double ouch, isn't it?!

It is not always black and white, though. In another case, the president was a graduate of our programme and told his HR director to get us to quote on some training. This is exciting, and you think "we are looking good." The president knows the quality and results from first-hand experience, and has the authority to make this happen. Or so it seems.

In this example, I actually did get to meet the HR people and their internal client. I followed up to present the proposal. "No, we are very busy, just send it." Warning signal right there. I pushed back, "Actually, I need to explain it for you." Further stalling. "No, just send it." The pricing, by the way, was very close to their indication.

Eventually, I sent it, but began to suspect this was HR's revenge on the president for daring to enter their world of authority. What looked like an inside track to a positive decision got derailed as the internal buying entity flexed their muscles to show their independence. Applying my standard rule, I did not follow up further and just waited to see what would happen. There was no response from their side, so again I was the patsy.

These things happen in business, but the key point is not to take it personally. Sales is a roller coaster ride of ups and downs, and your emotions are always under attack. Accept that sometimes you will get played by the buyer, but keep a record of the incident. Every six months, give that company a call to see if your nefarious counterpart is still working there.

People are much more mobile in Japan compared with many years ago, and there is a good chance that the puppeteer has moved on. We should not deal with that individual buyer again, but we can try to deal with the company. There are usually many buyers in your market, and many with whom you have had no contact; so there is little need to deal with bad buyer behaviour. As we say, "Fool me once it's your fault, fool me twice it's my fault."

ACTION STEPS

1. If you are in an industry where buyers habitually treat salespeople badly, switch industries.
2. Just because the people at the top like you, don't think that means anything in Japan. Keep working on those who execute the work.
3. If the buyer just says, "Send it to me," get worried. You may be the patsy unknowingly assisting a rival's offer.
4. Keep in touch with the company. The "problem child" may have moved on.
5. Never forget: "Fool me once it's your fault, fool me twice it's my fault."

In the next chapter, we will look at how to use storytelling sales to convince clients to buy.

24—Five-Step Storytelling for Salespeople

Salespeople must become the best communicators on the planet. Instinctively, we all know storytelling is a great communication tool, but the word itself is a problem. We associate it with bedtime stories, and therefore the idea sounds a bit childish. Hollywood talks about the "arc of the story." Media punishes politicians for the "lack of narrative." This is just storytelling dressed in more formal attire.

The other problem with storytelling is that we are not very good at it. It seems too simple. Anyone can tell a story! Ah ... but can they?

Stories come into their own when we use examples drawn from real work done for clients. How many really good stories have you heard from your fellow salespeople lately? Have they taken the client into a story that has them emotionally and logically involved? In my observation, many salespeople are untrained, poor communicators.

The Five-Step Storytelling process focuses on moving clients to action. We might tell our story in the first person, from the point of view of our own experience, or we may use the third person, referring to the insights of someone else, like a happy client.

1. Why?
We begin by clarifying the "Why." The story draws out the immediacy and relevance of the problem or issue. This is a critical step, because clients are surfing through hundreds of emails, Facebook and Twitter posts, LinkedIn updates, Instagram messages, etc. They are dealing with family, work, finances, and health issues. There is tremendous competition for their mind space. If we don't have a powerful "Why" to grab their attention, it's game over right there.

2. What?
The next step is to tell the client the "What." This is information they don't already have, or have not sufficiently focused on. This

will bring forth data or perspectives which are pertinent, immediate, and grip our client's attention.

Imparting key points—each linked to solid evidence—is essential, because we are all card-carrying sceptics. There is so much false information floating around in the sales world. Clients are permanently on guard against feeling cheated or being made to look foolish. We must communicate what they need to do to be successful. This might be our own recommendation or a happy-client story, told in the third person.

3. How?

Having isolated the issue and imparted evidence that provides a compelling reason to take the issue seriously, we now present the "How." This will explain in some detail what needs to be done to move forward, so that the listener can take immediate action.

4. What Ifs

We vanquish any client doubts or concerns by exploring the "What Ifs." We join the conversation going on in the client's mind about the fears they might have about what we are suggesting. We address these in the story, so that there are no or few residual barriers to taking action.

5. Action!

Finally, we outline the recommend "Action Steps," succinctly and clearly, so that these stay fresh in the client's mind. Compressing the steps into numbers like three, five, or seven works best, as they tend to be easily recalled. Few people can hold elaborate data points in their head. The storytelling mantra is:

> *Keep it short.*
> *Keep it memorable.*

This Five-Step Storytelling process incorporates the Why, What, How, What Ifs, and the Action needed to bring the client with us. Let's use evidence-rich stories from the work we have done for other clients to boost our persuasion power and make our solution more compelling.

ACTION STEPS
1. Plan your examples of success using stories about other clients.
2. Use the five steps to cover the Why, What, How, What Ifs, and Actions to be taken.

In the next chapter, we will look at things we may be doing which make it hard to get results.

25—Stop Killing Your Sales

W
hat we say and how we say it matters. It matters in life, in families, and in business. It especially matters in sales, where the talk is driven by semantics. But the classic Hollywood big-talking salesperson is an artefact, a dusty relic now banished to the tombs. Today, salespeople have to be articulate but not glib, concise but not flowery, evidence-based and not barrow-boy spivs.

Here are some typical sales fails:

1. Lack of Preparation
The first big fail is lack of preparation and anticipation of the issues facing the client. Because of this, the language being used is vague and often meandering.

Salespeople should complete a mini SWOT (Strength, Weaknesses, Opportunities, Threats) analysis on the industry and company to flag potential problems requiring solutions, and to direct the discussion to the elements of greatest interest to the buyer.

Of course, we need to be asking good questions to find out what the buyer needs. Using SWOT allows us to get to the key points faster and builds more credibility.

2. Blocker Words
Another killer of sales success is directly related to a lack of discipline. Salespeople go shooting off their mouths without engaging their brains, and in the process out pour words that scupper the deal.

What are blocker words? Common ones include: sort of, a few, kinda, sometimes, more or less, about, and some. All are vagaries to which no useful sales evidence can be attached. We should speak with authority and certainty, because clients want our full belief and commitment so that they can trust what we say is true.

Words like price, cost, and contract are also poor choices. These words create an image of money going out like a flood, but no value coming back in. We should only be speaking of value and investment.

Your parents told you to be careful about signing a contract, so let's sign an "agreement" instead. These are simple semantic switches in emphasis, but they make a big difference in what the client hears.

3. Talking Too Much

Salespeople love people and they love to chat. Too many words that add no value to the sales process pop into the conversation. Being concise is the key objective. Pare back the dialogue to only words which are relevant, project value, are laden with evidence, and build trust. Everything else must go.

Getting clients to hand over their hard-earned cash is difficult enough. Using poor communication skills makes it even harder. We need to monitor our sales conversations to make sure we are achieving the maximum success possible.

ACTION STEPS

1. Salespeople need to adopt the language of the client.
2. Don't allow laxity of word usage.
3. Be concise in verbal sales communication.

In the next chapter, we will look at why many Japanese companies are considered the gold standard in customer service.

26—Mr Kurokawa's Real Japanese Customer Service

To get some flavour of serving a customer Japanese style, let me tell you about Mr Kurokawa. As it turns out, I know Mr Kurokawa personally, because we are members of the same Rotary Club.

I am sure you have seen notices explaining that a building is going to close for reconstruction, and it will reopen on a specified date. Given the increasingly stringent earthquake building codes in Tokyo, we are seeing many businesses opting to rebuild their premises.

One notice, however, was much talked about amongst Japanese retailers. Toraya are a famous traditional Japanese sweets manufacturer and retailer, and Mr Mitsuhiro Kurokawa is the 17th generation of his family to lead the business. His "we are rebuilding" notice is considered outstanding, even in a country where *omotenashi*, or premium customer service, is much renowned.

Most relocation notices convey facts, supply relevant data, and provide the obligatory greetings about serving us again when they reopen. Mr Kurokawa did all of that, and much more. He put the current change in historical perspective, noting the business started in Kyoto in 1586 toward the end of the Muromachi Period (1338–1573), moved to Tokyo in 1869, and settled in the current location in 1964.

By doing this, he is assuring us of their traditions, longevity, and capacity to change with the times. He also shared stories about the customers who have visited this shop on Aoyama Street in Akasaka over the past 51 years.

Every three days, one story goes, a male customer visited to enjoy *oshiruko* (sweet red bean soup with grilled *mochi*, or rice cake). This is considered a bit unusual in Japan. Men don't normally have such a sweet tooth, so this customer stood out.

Another customer, a kindergarten-aged boy, came to the shop with his mother every day and bought a bite-sized *yookan* (sweet bean paste block). One day, he came by himself. The staff were worried about him, so they went out with him and found that the mother was hiding and watching to be sure he was okay.

There was also a 100-year-old lady who regularly came to the shop by wheelchair. She later became hospitalised, and her family came to buy *namagashi* (fresh Japanese sweets) and *higashi* (dried sugar sweet) for her. Even after she could no longer eat, they found that she could still enjoy her favourite dried sweets if they crushed them.

Mr Kurokawa mentioned that he couldn't include all the episodes they have shared with their customers over the past 51 years, but said that he and the staff keep them, one by one, in their hearts forever.

Telling customer stories is powerful. Mr Kurokawa made the experiences of Toraya's customers come alive, and he linked them to the products the company sells.

Rather than just a cold statement of facts, he crafted a message of love for his customers. The feeling of the notice is that Toraya has a special bond with all its customers; and even though they won't reopen on that site for three years, they won't have forgotten them, and look forward to serving them forever.

As salespeople, are we communicating that we feel a special bond with our customers? Often, corporate communications become machine-like, wrapped up in what can sound like marketing department dross.

Mr Kurokawa conveys a lot of heartfelt emotion in this simple notice. Are we weaving enough customer stories into our company's marketing communications? I don't mean fake propaganda stories, but real episodes that the reader can visualise in their mind's eye.

Toraya's notice gets attention in Japan because of the sincerity of the message. It epitomises the spirit of a family that has served customers for 17 generations.

We may not be working for the 17th generation in our firm, but we can bring more heart to the service we provide. We can start right now to change how we communicate that service.

ACTION STEPS
1. Are we really thinking about creating an emotional connection with our clients?
2. Are we telling enough happy client stories in our communications?
3. Are we fully aware of the content of all the touch points we have with our buyers?
4. Are we serving from the heart or just the head?
5. Are we instilling the right frame of reference into our staff, regarding how to properly serve the client?

In the next chapter, we will work on our sales presentation skills.

27—Presentation Skills for Salespeople

Being persuasive is a must when convincing buyers to give up their security (money) in exchange for the promise of higher value. Surprisingly, very few salespeople have had any presentation training whatsoever. We are basically making it up as we go, doing the best we can; that is to say, a fairly mediocre job.

Given that there are so many great courses and books available on presenting, you have to wonder why the two dots are not being connected? Let me try to reverse that trend and throw some light on the subject.

The basics of presenting to an audience or a buyer are the same. It could be one-to-one or one-to-many, but there are necessary skills that are common to both. Let's start with the Six Impact Points of Persuasion Power.

EYES

If we are talking to a buyer group, a board, or a few representatives from a department within the client company, we need to engage each of them with eye contact. Holding someone's gaze for about six seconds allows us to make our point with becoming intrusive.

Too little eye contact is meaningless, but too much is confronting. Hold their gaze for six seconds as you make your key point, then move to the next person and continue. Keep repeating this pattern throughout the entire talk.

When you make eye contact, focus both of your eyes on just one of theirs. We cannot focus on two objects at the same time. If we try, the power of our eye contact becomes diffused. Go for a single point of focus.

In Japan, if we are with just one person, continuous eye contact can become too much. Break off and look away from time to time to give them a break. By the way, move your whole head, not just your eyes—otherwise you can come across as shifty and untrustworthy.

As mentioned, Japanese buyers can feel oppressed by strong eye contact. You should still make eye contact, but do it much more sparingly. Usually, in Japan, the meeting is attended by two or more people from the buyer's side, so you can switch your eye contact back and forth between them.

Japanese people are trained to look at the chin, the forehead, and the throat rather than make strong eye contact. In a Western context, the inability to make direct eye contact is taken as a sign of untrustworthiness and is a negative. In Japan, if someone doesn't make eye contact with you, don't make assumptions about trustworthiness.

Japan doesn't have that same context, so you can relax about making continuous eye contact. It is not all or nothing. It is more nuanced. Still, when you want to emphasise a key point, make eye contact to add weight to your words.

If you are giving a more formal presentation to a group, definitely use eye contact; but only for that maximum of six seconds. Over the course of your talk, eye contact should be made with as many people in the group as possible, selecting people in six sectors of the audience. Which six sectors?

Think of a baseball diamond. You have left, centre, and right field, plus infield and outfield. This creates a six-sector split, and you want to make eye contact with people sitting in all six sectors, one by one. Sometimes you see speakers who neglect half their audience because of the way they are standing, or they only engage the front of the room and ignore everyone at the back. Engage everyone—but don't do it in linear order. Make it random. If you do it in any perceptible order, your audience can tell when you will be looking at them. All the other sector groups immediately switch off and you lose their attention.

You might imagine that you only need to make eye contact with the obvious decision-maker and can ignore all the troops. Japan can be a mysterious place when it comes to who exactly makes the decision, so the single-person strategy is not a good one.

The group involvement means everyone will have some input, to block or possibly to agree. Blocking is preferred regarding anything new or with any possibility of risk. The new and risky is usually you, because they see that you want to create a new client. Therefore, assume you must win everyone over to your idea, not just the big boss in the room.

FACE

A wooden face, devoid of expression, may be great for poker; but is not great for convincing clients to buy our product or service. Remember, sales is a transfer of our enthusiasm for the solution to the buyer. Yet, many salespeople have a single expression throughout the sales conversation. They never tap into this wonderful opportunity to align inner belief in the value of what is being offered with the outward expression of that belief.

Our face, when animated, lends powerful support to our message. When something is great for the client, smile and show pleasure. When something is bad for the client (like taking no action and not buying), show some downheartedness at the thought of the client not getting the wonderful benefits of your solution.

Japanese salespeople and buyers can be animated, too, but this usually comes after you have built up enough trust for them to feel they can relax a little bit when with you. Their guard is not down, but they can become noticeably more relaxed than at the start of the meeting. They become especially animated over drinks and dinner at night!

VOICE

Monotone sounds put us to sleep. Tonal modulation makes our voice a fantastic instrument. Classical music is full of powerful crescendos and lulls in the storm. The opposite natures of these musical interludes make the contrast so much more powerful.

We don't have to be that melodramatic, but we need to have contrast when we speak. Sometimes we want to speak almost at a whisper to draw our client in to hear what we are saying.

At other times, we want to be very strong—not loud, but strong—to drive home an important point.

When I teach the High Impact Presentation's Course, Japanese people often tell me they are at a disadvantage, because their language is monotone, without the tonal variations of English. This is not the case.

There may be no similar tonal variations available in the Japanese language, but there are two powerful levers that create vocal contrast: power and speed.

Injecting power when we say something, or taking the power down to almost a whisper, is also a clever variation in delivery.

Slowing words down for emphasis works in any language. Speeding them up also works well to set what we are saying apart from all the other words surrounding it.

Fast delivery in Japanese, with a foreign accent, can be challenging for Japanese clients. This tends to be one of my problems. I speak too quickly in Japanese, and my Aussie accent can sometimes make me hard to understand. And let's not talk about my mastery of Japanese grammar!

We might also become nervous or excited, and suddenly start speeding up without realising it.

Apart from sections where you want to add power or speed for emphasis, always keep it at a slowish, even pace—especially if you are doing this in English. Their English might sound pretty good, but if your delivery is too quick, Japanese buyers may struggle to keep up with where you are going with the story.

Speed is critical, so keep regular tabs on yourself to make sure your speaking speed isn't too fast for your audience.

Being very polite, they won't necessarily ask you to repeat yourself or ask about what you just said. You think you are on a roll and become even more excited and speed up. Slow down!

Also, avoid idioms as much as possible when presenting to Japanese buyers. Those favourite idioms of yours will be impenetrable to the buyer. As an Aussie, this is a constant struggle, because we seem to be the idiom headquarters of the world!

GESTURES

Gestures come more easily when we are standing rather than sitting. At most business meetings I have attended, the participants were seated. However, if you must present something, stand up and do it. This could be done using a whiteboard, a flip chart, or a slide deck on a screen.

Even if you have no visual aids to support you when presenting—if it is a formal presentation like a pitch—still stand up and give your report. When standing, we can make more use of our body language, can make full use of our hands for gesturing, and are more visible to all members of the audience, no matter where they are seated. Plus, we are more relaxed.

More relaxed? Well, maybe not when you first get up, but as you get into it, you will find you can relax. The standing helps to create movement (don't sway though) and burns off some of that nervous energy. Remember, only you know that you are nervous; so keep it to yourself and don't let anyone else know what you are feeling inside.

In a Japanese business meeting context, salespeople rarely stand to give their presentations. Whenever I am doing workshops, and sometimes even for public speeches, the organisers have kindly prepared a desk, a low microphone stand, and a chair for me. This is very standard in Japan. You see it all the time—someone seated, reading their speech and just droning on and on and on, just killing everyone in the audience. I get rid of the desk and chair, and stand so I can bring all my persuasion power to my message.

By the way, the seller standing up, above the buyer, puts the hierarchy the wrong way around in a Japanese context. This is not a problem, as long as you apologise for standing (because otherwise it implies some sense of superiority over the buyer), and then explain that it will make for a better presentation.

Foreigners are given some leeway in Japan and are not expected to conform to all aspects of business culture, including this instance. Apologise for standing, politely ignore any entreaties to be seated, and then get into it. What normally happens is the

Japanese business audience is reminded how much better foreigners are at presenting than they are.

We can also gesture from a seated position—and we should. Don't allow seating arrangements to constrict you. Use your hands to emphasise a point in coordination with your voice and facial expressions. This troika is a powerful weapon in the persuasion battle.

Whether standing or seated, never maintain the same gesture for more than 15 seconds. When teaching presentations skills, I notice some people never use any gestures, whereas others use the same one throughout.

If we hold a position for more than 15 seconds, the power of the gesture dies and it just becomes annoying to the audience. Like a faucet, we need to turn our gestures on and then turn them off again. This will keep the gesture fresh and maintain its power for giving greater emphasis to key points.

PAUSE

Salespeople love to talk. In fact, we love it so much we forget to shut up. We just keep talking and talking and talking. Never forget this point: If you ever find yourself doing all the talking in a meeting with the buyer, then SHUT UP!

We want the client to do most of the talking, guided by our well-designed questions. If we are hogging the limelight, then the balance is out of kilter and we are making it incredibly hard for ourselves to make the sale. When we are nervous, we tend to speed up and just keep blathering away. We need discipline to stop ourselves and allow the client to tell us what they need.

Foreigners are also more self-conscious about gaps in the conversation—signified by silence—and feel compelled to "rescue" the situation by continuing to occupy the airwaves! Always remember: Japanese are perfectly at ease with silence.

We need to introduce gaps in the conversation using pauses, because the client must be given a chance to absorb what we have just said. This means they shouldn't have to listen to anything we are saying now in competition with what we have just said.

We tend to roll one new idea right over the top of the last one. Soon, the client can't recall what we said five minutes ago.

When we keep adding a new piece of information immediately after the last, the client struggles to follow the point. We are making it hard for them to focus on the key points, which are usually our most persuasive and powerful. Pause, remain quiet, and let your key points sink in before continuing. Embrace the beauty of the pause.

POSTURE

If seated, sit tall. Foreigners are much less formal than Japanese and, without knowing it, can breach cultural norms. We are given some leeway, because we are not Japanese, but posture is one of those simple things we can manage to get right from a cultural perspective.

Don't cross your legs or your ankles, and certainly don't sprawl in your chair. I have seen plenty of all three—including the latter heinous crime—when attending meetings between Japanese buyers and foreign sellers. The more formal the meeting, the more formal the posture. Take a good look at how the buyers are seated. This will be a good guide to what you need to do.

We are here to convey reliability, trust, consistency, and attention to detail. A slob collapsed in their chair isn't likely to succeed on that front. Unfortunately, no one will ever take you aside and wise you up. They won't say a thing, and you'll just keep murdering your potential to establish a positive first impression.

Japanese culture dictates that you sit ramrod straight and off the backrest of the chair. It is very similar to the ancient rules of patrician Roman culture and, for the same reason, conveys dignity and respect.

If standing, then stand tall. As foreigners, yes, as I mentioned, we do get cut some slack over cultural norms; but posture is one of those things we had best match with the culture instead of dismissing as pointless.

For centuries, how samurai should walk, sit, arise, bow, and stand were all set down in great detail. We still see it today in all the Japanese martial arts, and in traditional arts such as calligraphy, *ikebana*, and tea ceremony. This expectation of correct posture on the part of the seller is still there in the deep recesses of the buyer's mind.

So, when standing, that means both legs are kept straight, shoulder width apart (ladies a little less than shoulder width). Spreading your weight across your legs 60/40 or 70/30 looks far too casual and relaxed for a business meeting—especially when you are the supplicant salesperson. Spread your weight 50/50 across your legs and stand as tall as you can.

PRESENTING OUR SALES MATERIALS

If we are presenting a brochure, flyer, price list, hard-copy slide deck, or any other typical collateral item, then we should adopt best practices for greatest success. Have two copies always—one for you to read and one for the client—unless you are a genius of reading upside down, which, by the way, all Japanese seem to be!

At the start, put your copy to the side, in case you need it later, and turn the client's copy around to face them. Then proceed to physically control the page turns.

Don't just hand it over, if you can avoid it. You want to walk them through the pages, under strict supervision. There is usually a lot of information involved, and we only want to draw attention to the key points. We don't receive unlimited time, so we have to plan well.

If it is one of those monster boardroom tables, where the distance between you and the buyer is massive, then try to sit at the end of the table on the corner, so that you can get closer to the buyer to guide them through the presentation. If that is not possible, then refer them to specific pages and do the guiding remotely; but still do the guiding. You don't want the buyer to be on page eight when you are still on page one.

By the way, don't place any collateral pieces in view of the client at the start of the meeting. Keep them out of sight on the chair next to you or in your bag. Why? We want to spend the first part of the meeting asking solid questions to uncover the client's needs.

Then we mentally scan the solution library in our brain and start lining up products for them. The details will be in a brochure or a flyer, etc. If we show these items at the start, we will distract the client. Displaying sales material also implies, "I am here to sell you something." What is our mantra?

> **"**
>
> *Everyone loves to buy,*
> *but nobody wants to be sold to.*
> *Keep the sales materials out of sight*
> *until you know what you will need.*
>
> **"**

Also, at the beginning, we don't know which materials to show. Are they after blue or pink? There is no point in going to great depths to describe your unmatchable pink if they only want to buy blue. After the questioning phase is complete, we know what they want—and only then can we grab our materials and guide them through the details.

If we hand over the sales materials at the start, the buyer will be distracted by the details. If this happens, control of the sales conversation has been lost. The salesperson's key job is to keep control of the sales talk direction, from beginning to end. If you can't do that, then selling is going to be a tough employ.

After placing the document in front of the buyer, facing them, pick up your nice pen and use it to show them where to look. There are so many distractions on any single page, so we need to keep the show on the road and the buyer focused only on the key items.

When we need to make a strong point, we should back it up by using eye contact. To get their eyes off the page, so they can make eye contact with us, simply raise the pen to your own eye level and their gaze will soon join yours. Remember, six seconds maximum.

Know where all items are in your materials so that you can focus on those of most interest, based on what you heard earlier, and skip pages that are not as relevant. Do not go through the whole thing from beginning to end. You just don't have that much time.

SLIDE DECKS

The preparation of slide decks is a very specific "visual" topic, so please visit the Dale Carnegie Training Japan YouTube channel. We have a comprehensive video tutorial covering all the nitty-gritty detail of what works best.

In the playlists, there is a section called "How to Become Really Excellent at Presentations." Scroll down to find the video titled "How to Use PowerPoint, etc., (Properly) When Presenting."

This takes you through colours, fonts, graphs, tables, photos, layout—everything you need to know in one place.

When it comes to getting these details wrong, the Japanese are currently at world-champion level. Everything and the kitchen sink is thrown up on the one screen, with garish colours and disparate fonts. Usually, it is a total mess.

Don't make this your template in an effort to blend in. The country of zen has not yet managed to apply minimalism to what goes up on a screen. With onscreen presentations, the basic rule is "less is more."

If the data is very detailed—especially with lots of rows and columns filled with numbers—you are much better off distributing those pages separately.

PROPOSAL DOCUMENTS

In Japan, it is extremely rare that we wrap up a deal at the first meeting. Usually, we come back with our solution and pricing. There are many favoured standard styles for presenting proposals to clients, so there is no need to go through all of them in this book.

However, in general, most Japanese buyers have a tremendous desire for detail.

When I was a student here in the late 1970s, I attended an international symposium on Sino-Japanese relations. One of the Japanese academics was relaying a story about the introduction of zen to Japan from China. One of the zen stories used a well and a bucket as a metaphor for a spiritual point of instruction. In the Chinese version, the key point was the allegory, not the detail of the equipment being used.

In the Japanese version, great attention was placed on the dimensions of the well, the bucket, the winding mechanism, the construction of the rope, etc. I have never forgotten that insight, and it has played out as a truism here in Japan. I have found it is almost impossible to give the Japanese buyer too much detail.

This is part of their risk aversion preference. By having more and more detail, they can reduce the possibility of a mistake or failure. They will suck up as much detail as they can get out of you.

This doesn't mean that you should give them so much detail, because it diffuses their concentration on the key things we want them to focus on. Remember, we should never sell past the sale. However, bear in mind that the buyer's demand for detail and data is always going to be super strong.

The proposal should reflect the information captured during the sales interview. Outline what you believe to be the issue facing the client, based on what they told you. It is critical to check that you have clearly understood their needs.

If this is incorrect, the rest of the document is immediately headed for the trash. Assuming this is not the case, and you have accurately laid out that understanding, now suggest your solution.

Depending on your preference, you can present the content in this way:

Expected Result–Problem–Solution
or
Problem–Solution–Expected Result

At the solution explanation point, go into substantial detail.

Where possible, try not to just send the proposal document by email. Present it yourself, because what may have been clear to you when you composed it may not be so clear to the buyer when they read it. We often assume knowledge that the other person doesn't have, and so key points can be missed.

Sometimes, buyers will say, "Just email me the proposal." Resist this idea with every fibre in your body. Get over there and present it instead. Mention that you have something you must "show them," and explain that this is why you can't just send it.

Sales is all about presenting ideas, insights, solutions, new information, and value to the buyer. We therefore need to become absolute experts in the delivery of that information. Get presentation training. High Impact Presentations is a phenomenal two-day course, which I strongly recommend. This is the Rolls Royce of presentation training, and building these skills is how you lift yourself above the competition.

ACTION STEPS

1. Get training in presentation skills and stop kidding yourself.
2. After you get training, always keep polishing your presentation skills

In the next chapter, we will cover how to motivate ourselves when we are exhausted from last year and have new and higher targets for this year.

28—The Danger Zone: The New Financial Year

In Greek mythology, Sisyphus, king of Corinth, was banished to Hades for misdeeds in life and spent eternity repeatedly rolling a large stone to the top of a hill, only to watch it tumble back down. This is the sales life. At the end of each financial year, or quarter, we are back down at the bottom of the hill. Here we go again, having to push that big rock all the way to the top.

"You are only as good as your last deal." This is a common refrain in sales (usually from the sales manager). We struggle all year to hit our targets, and then find ourselves back at zero, starting to roll those massive KPI rocks up the hill once more.

Most salespeople struggle to hit their targets. Even if they do, the targets are always being raised again anyway. The effort to get deals over the line before the cut-off point, leaves us in a dishevelled heap. We go to bed one night utterly exhausted, only to arise the next morning to find an even bigger rock facing us. We are already tired, so how do we motivate ourselves to get into the game again?

Maybe we hit our target. Maybe we didn't. It doesn't matter, because now we are in a new financial year and revenue is back at zero. We brothers and sisters of sales have to start again.

Learn from the Past (but Leave It Behind)

So, the first thing is to not worry about the past. Draw lessons from it, but don't allow yesterday's result to intimidate today's attitude. You lost some good clients, sweet deals, or potential revenue sources? That was last year. Now you have a whole new year to do better. Switch your thinking to the current year and don't repeat the lost battles of the past. Our mind is a powerful thing, but we have to program it properly.

Control What Goes into Your Mind

Fill your mind with thoughts of peace, courage, health, and hope. We cannot tolerate a vacuum in our minds, so either the good stuff goes in or we allow the bad stuff to disable us. We should not dwell on the negatives, but concentrate on finding solutions to our clients' problems.

Oh no! We find out that our biggest client won't be buying this year, and that is going to leave a massive hole in our numbers. Japan has a job rotation system in larger companies. That nice Mr. Suzuki, who has been such a brilliant client, is being trundled off to some remote outpost, which means your strong connection is being severed. The new person is not helpful, and the business is not going to continue.

Don't moan about it. Start work on finding new, wonderful clients to replace the lost one. Get on to positive momentum to carry you forward. Your *kokorogamae*—or true intention—is to help as many clients as possible, because—unlike 99% of your competition—you deliver real value. In this vein, you are never shy to find more people you can help, and you know there are always a lot of people who need help. You still have your sanity—and that is rather useful in a profession like sales, which can sometimes drive you nuts. So, be thankful and get on to it.

Decide to Become Healthier This Year
Sales is a stressful occupation, an emotional rollercoaster that can quickly spin out of control. Make sure you maintain your health by adjusting what you eat and drink. We all know what we are supposed to do, we just don't do it. Well, this year, do it!

Also, while the food we put into our mouths is important, so is what we put into our minds. Control the data flowing into your head and try to keep exposure to the negative news cycle to a minimum. Read content that makes you feel happier or smarter. Finding out about some disgusting incident that occurred some-where yesterday is not uplifting, helpful, or nourishing for the brain. This describes almost all the news being beamed into our lives by media outlets.

Become more proactive and positive instead. Study what you know you should be studying, but for which, so far, you have neglected to allocate the required time. Aimlessly staring into blue screens to consume social media, television, or internet content, is usually not study.

Allocate time for learning each day, and be disciplined about doing it. Your brain will be on fire with ideas and possibilities. The big target-number rock will no longer be seen as a terror.

Expect Ingratitude
If you expect ingratitude, you become bulletproof, because bad news and bad behaviour never catch you mentally unprepared. Your client chooses your competitor despite the close relationship you have. Typically, you feel like you are dealing with an unfaithful spouse and are burning up with rage. If you assume that ingratitude is the usual state of the world, then you just brush it off and move forward. That good client of yours will be back at some point, so don't blow the relationship over one deal gone missing.

Count Your Blessings, Not Your Troubles
You are focused on the hill and the rock, but not on your strengths. You have experience, contacts, a track record, and a good reputation in the marketplace. You are a professional who always has the client's interests as your first priority. You practice your craft and you study to improve. There are always more potential clients than time available to service them, so there is no lack of prospects. Your competitors are not studying as hard and typically don't have the client's interests at heart. This gives you an advantage over the long term, as they just flame out and disappear.

Try to Profit from Your Losses
Not every post is a winner, despite your best efforts. I love this saying, another mantra:

> **“**
> *All you can do, is all you can do.*
> *But all you can do is enough.*
> **”**

If you are doing your best every single day, you will be successful. The hills and valleys of inconsistent enthusiasm are where we get off track.

Winston Churchill has a great quote related to this, and let me repeat it here again for you because it really nails the challenge of the sales life:

> **Success consists of going from failure to failure without loss of enthusiasm.**

Failure is the nature of sales—it is built into the activity—so we have to deal with this reality. Analyse what went wrong. Don't be afraid to ask the client for feedback.

Our experience is the sum of our failures. We learn what works by finding out what doesn't. In the start-up world, they have the touchstone "fail faster." This is an old idea. Thomas Edison applied this same concept to discover which materials would bridge the gap in his electric bulb. See your sales future like this:

> **Excellent! We have another fresh start to get it right this year.**

Create Happiness for Others

Give something back. Provide advice, mentor, volunteer, turn up, and help. When we give, we receive much more in return. Our soul is warmed by the act and our spirit is strengthened.

Join the PTA board, the chamber committee, the charity ball organising group. Turn up at events for worthy causes. You will feel good about yourself and meet nice, like-minded people. Some of them may even become clients!

Break that Big Number Down

Rather than confronting that massive, ugly annual-target boulder that scares the pants off you, reduce it. Get that big, hideous numeral down to bite-sized pieces. What is the daily number you need to be aiming for to hit that annualised target?

If you know your ratios—how many calls attempted, how many prospects spoken to, how many met, average size of transaction—you are in a good place to make calculations. Your target number must be translated into your daily activity profile. If you have to produce revenue of "x," how many people do you need to call each day to get there. Simple mathematics are very necessary to get our minds off our fears and on to generating results.

Don't be overwhelmed by the hill in front of you. Break it down to centimetres and roll that rock a little each and every day. You will get to the top.

Okay, we have to start over, but that is the fun of the game. We get to play again and see what we can do this year, which wonderful new clients we can help, what creative solutions we can generate. We are awesomely powerful learning machines, and the game is our university of life.

ACTION STEPS

1. Don't worry about the past.
2. Fill your mind with thoughts of peace, courage, health, and hope.
3. Expect ingratitude.
4. Count your blessings, not your troubles.
5. Try to profit from your losses.
6. Create happiness for others.

Time to wrap it all up in the Conclusion, our final chapter.

Conclusion

Sales is simple and complex at the same time. If you don't know what you are doing, it is diabolical. Why so many salespeople around the world opt for the diabolical is beyond me. In sales, some things work better than others; and we should do those things. There are ways of dealing with people that work better than others. We should do those, too.

Follow the sales process and philosophy outlined in this book, and you will definitely be more successful. We are all standing on the shoulders of sales giants, and we have accumulated so much knowledge about sales as a profession. This knowledge is readily available. Only our patience and effort are at risk.

Yes, Japan is different, special, unique. It is also wonderful. It has rule of law, politeness, order, consideration, safety, honesty, wealth, and sophistication. You get paid in Japan, people are reliable, things work here. It is currently wide open to the sales professional, because there are so few skilled rivals.

Most Japanese and foreigners selling in Japan have no idea what they are doing. They are not getting trained properly at work and are not being led properly by their bosses.

This spells opportunity for those who want to "seize the day." Why not be part of that group?

Final mantra:

> *Get your kokorogamae right,*
> *become totally fluent in your sales process,*
> *and the sales world will be right for you—*
> *be it in Japan or anywhere else. If you can*
> *make it here, you can make it anywhere!*

ABOUT THE AUTHOR

Dr Greg Story is a sixth-generation Australian born in Brisbane, Queensland. His first job after high school was selling Encyclopaedia Britannica door to door. He was a total failure in sales. After four years of working in various "dirty, dangerous, and difficult" jobs, he saved enough money to put himself through university.

Graduating with honours in Modern Asian Studies at Griffith University, he came to Japan in 1979 on scholarship from the Japanese Ministry of Education, Science and Culture. During that first four-year tour, he began the study of Japanese and completed a Master's Degree at Jochi University in Tokyo. He returned in 1984 to begin field work for his doctorate as a Japan Foundation Fellow. He was later awarded his PhD from Griffith University in Queensland.

After establishing his own consulting business—the Japan Business Consultancy—he resumed his sales career. In 1989, he was recruited by Jones Lang Wootton in Brisbane to run their Japan Desk, selling office buildings, shopping malls, five-star hotels, and golf courses to Japanese corporates.

In 1992, he returned to Japan with the Australian Trade and Investment Commission (Austrade) to establish a startup sales operation in Nagoya. In 1996, he took over Austrade Osaka and, in 2001, he ran Austrade Tokyo, later becoming country head for Austrade in Japan.

In 2003, he joined the Shinsei Retail Bank with instructions to turn around the sales team, which was tasked with selling investment products to wealthy Japanese individuals. In 2007, he became country head for the National Australia Bank in Japan, again focused on financial investment products.

In that same year, he and his partners bought the franchise rights for Dale Carnegie Training in Japan. In 2010, he left the National Australia Bank to work in the Dale Carnegie Training business as its Japan president.

He is a sixth dan in traditional shitoryu karate. This is his 46th year of karate training, during which time he has been an international athlete, coach, referee, and official. His other great sporting passion is rugby, and he supports the Brisbane Broncos, the Queensland State of Origin Team, the Kangaroos, the Queensland Reds, and the Wallabies.

The Sales Advantage Course

What Does This Course Deliver?

Teach you how to become a "shoot the lights out" <u>sales professional</u>

How Does It Do That?

It triggers five major shifts in your sales approach

- Build Real Belief In Yourself
- Become Major Value For Your Buyers
- Master Consultative Selling
- Create Client Loyalty & Lifetime Value
- Produce <u>Big Numbers</u>

Course Availability

It is running all the time
Delivered in Japanese and English

Dale Carnegie Training Japan

TEL: 0120-987-099, 03-4520-5470 weekdays 9:00 18:00, closed Sat/Sun/Holidays

FAX: 03-4520-5483

DALECARNEGIE.COM

Leadership Training For Managers

What Does This Course Deliver?

Teach you how to become the leader people <u>want to follow</u>

How Does It Do That?

It triggers five major shifts in your leadership

- Create Your Personal Leadership Sweet Spot
- Achieve Massive Leverage Through Your Team
- Produce Super Innovation
- Build "Crawl Over Broken Glass" Loyal Followers
- Drive Consistently <u>Big Results</u>

Course Availability

It is running all the time
Delivered in Japanese and English

Dale Carnegie Training Japan

TEL: 0120-987-099, 03-4520-5470 weekdays 9:00 18:00, closed Sat/Sun/Holidays

FAX: 03-4520-5483

DALECARNEGIE.COM

Dale Carnegie

High-Impact Presentation Course

What Does This Course Deliver?

Teach you how to be <u>a star</u>!

How Does It Do That?

It triggers five major shifts in your presentation's approach

- Builds Massive Self Belief & Confidence
- Achieve Incredible Levels Of Persuasive Power
- Become The Speaker Everyone Wants To Hear <u>Again</u>
- Combine Quality Content With Unmatched Delivery Skills
- Own The Room

Course Availability

It is running all the time
Delivered in Japanese and English

Dale Carnegie Training Japan

TEL: 0120-987-099, 03-4520-5470 weekdays 9:00 18:00, closed Sat/Sun/Holidays

FAX: 03-4520-5483

DALECARNEGIE.COM

Dale Carnegie

Dale Carnegie Course®

Effective Communications & Human Relations

What Does This Course Deliver?

This course will <u>change your life</u> and produce a much improved you!

How Does It Do That?

It triggers five major shifts in your life

- Become Super Confident
- Ace Your Communication
- Become A Real Leader
- Obtain Awesome People Skills
- Totally Control Your Stress

Course Availability

It is running all the time
Delivered in Japanese and English

Dale Carnegie Training Japan

TEL: 0120-987-099, 03-4520-5470 weekdays 9.00 18.00, closed Sat/Sun/Holidays

FAX: 03-4520-5483

DALECARNEGIE.COM

Dale Carnegie

Made in the USA
Columbia, SC
14 February 2022

55700317R00117